Wealthy
in a Poverty Estate

Faith is More
than Important...

By Demetrius Smith

Tate Publishing, LLC

Acknowledgements

I give honor to my Lord and Savior Jesus Christ for His compassionate love He has given to me. I would like to thank my dad, James Mims for being the dad I never had, and the pastor that I needed. I love you graciously. I thank all of my mothers for the resounding love they have shown me; Devella, Rose, and Joyce. Devella, no one can ever replace you; without you, there is no me. Rose you are my lamp of love. Joyce you are the epitome of what a virtuous woman is all about.

I would like to let my grandparents know that they are forever appreciated for the foundation they have laid and the encouragement that they give; H.B. and Dora Smith, and Morris and Genetta Brown

To my current pastor, the honorable Bishop T.D. Jakes, thank you for your obedience to Christ. You are a profound example for many. I thank God for using you to confirm many things that I have written. Some things I struggled with, but the following Sunday you would speak about those specific things. I dare not to separate you from the first Lady, Serita, who is gracefully assisting you complete your tasks; and whose price is also far above rubies. Thank you, Bishop, I appreciate you, man!

To Detra, Dontae, Danissa, Eric, Erica, Ebony, and Ernie, and James Jr.—I love you all and thank God that I have you as my brothers and sisters. To Mr. Charles and Inez Wright, I haven't forgotten about your love, encouragement, and accepting me the way you have. Mr. and Mrs. Harold Akism, I need you to stay strong and keep encouragement riding on the surface of your tongue. I love you my friend(s)!

I send a special thanks to Tate Publishing and the entire Tate Publishing family for the effort and hard work they have put into this project. I thank God for the vision He has given you. A special thanks must be given to Dr. Richard Tate. Thank you, Dr. Tate, for your compassion, understanding, help, support, and faith in this project. I love you all with the love of Christ!

There are so many other people I want to thank. If I fail to mention any of you, just know that you support lingers in my heart.

Lastly, to my audience: I love you with the love of Christ!

Table Contents

Foreword 7

Preface - You want more 11

The Beginnings–Chapter 1 19
    -The capacity to understand

Covenant Keeper–Chapter 2 37
    -Faces
    -Sum total
    -God can't lie

A Balanced Beam–Chapter 3 59
    -Molded through the pressures of life
    -You need a seed
    -Built through battles

Faithastrophy–Chapter 4 79
    -Sustaining faith
    -Exercise your weakness
    -Disconnect the connection
    -The battle ground

Who is Exempt? Chapter 5 101
    -A deceptive power
    -A change in trust
    -Wealthy without completion

The Gardner - Chapter 6 123
    -Excess fat
    -Gardening for glory
    -Romantic devoir

Kingdom Building–Chapter 7 143
    -Internal cleansing
    -Made for His purpose
    -The end result

Revelation of Holy Things–Chapter 8 167
    -A holy thing
    -Unconditional love
    -Faith in what He says

A living Dead Man–Chapter 9 191
    -A walking miracle
    -Transformation
    -Metamorphosis
    -Believing what can't be seen -Expose'

Consummation–Chapter 10 217
    -Benefits of a made decision
    -He is more than much
    -Fulfilling the beginning

Foreword

As Christians living in this world and not of this world, Apostle Paul said *"Beware lest anyone cheat you through philosophy and empty deceit, according to the tradition of men, and not according to Christ (Colossians 2:8)."* We must return to the basic fundamental principles of the Word of God. We should be weaned from the milk only to desire meaty food from the Word of God. If we are new babes in Christ then we should desire the milk until we are able to understand and swallow the meat. What is being said here is that we need to do away with "entertaining" one another with the Gospel of Jesus Christ, and get back to the true foundation of why the Gospel was recorded. We need to go back to the basic fundamentals to establish a true foundation to build our understanding on. Then we should develop a keen desire to increase in our growth and understanding. Just as a baby must be nourished with the first level of drinking and eating milk until she grows into a stage to where she can eat meat, we must do likewise in our growth with God and His Word. This book serves as a compass pointing us in the right direction.

We must deviate from quick fix, name it claim it, get rich quick gimmicks and become deeply rooted on the biblical principles of true prosperity. We must strike a balance in the bodily and spiritual riches. Brother Demetrius' teachings and revelations in this book will stir up the gifts within us to see ourselves as God sees us and strive to acquire not only the corruptible, but also the incorruptible riches of God.

This book provides the key(s) to spiritual breakthrough with an in-depth study on how to walk by faith and not by sight. It teaches us on how to be totally God dependent in our pursuits in life. This book also offers some practical gems on how to live a successful and productive life. These gems include but not limited to: Prayer, Incessant passion for the Word of God, power of unity, team spirit, and a hunger for spiritual gifts.

The ingredients inside this book will galvanize and mobilize gallant armies for the Lord in the 21st century. Our generation needs this to survive and conquer the atrocities of the evil power that permeates the world today. The theme of this book is to ignite the zeal that already exists inside of you and help provide you the endurance to run the race set before you to the finish line, and to finish your race successfully. "Wealthy in a Poverty Estate" will imbue you with holy indignation needed to fight violently to regain all grounds lost to the enemy. You will become armed and dangerous with spiritual weapons needed to retaliate against any artillery launched at you by the demonic forces of the enemy.

This book was hatched out of Brother Demetrius' passion for prayer, the Word of God, and his passion for global salvation of sinners. I have watched him live what he has written inside this book, and I can assure you that experience is the best teacher. Demetrius writes to you out of his experiences. I strongly recommend this book as a must read for all with a hunger for God, for Christians who thirst for more of God, and for those aspiring to reach their potential, purpose, and destiny in life.

Reverend Johnson Obamehinti

Preface

Are you living without fulfillment in life? How many times have people encouraged you with words that God would bless you, and you still don't see those spoken effects over your life? Has life, seemingly, stripped you out of your majestic robe to leave you wallowing in pain? Are you so broken in your life that it makes you wonder what else could go wrong? I could ask you multiple questions until I weave my way into your life, but I won't.

I have been elected by God to give you a word that will help you quicken your dead relationship with Him. Even if you do not feel like your relationship is dead, this book will help you *fine-tune* your relationship with God.

The life we live demands that we constantly nourish our lives with God. Believe it or not, this is the only way for us to obtain total fulfillment; especially in the day we are living.

We are living in a day when we constantly hear about prosperity. Make no doubt about it—God has been moving to prosper His people, in spite of, adverse circumstances. We know about the catastrophe one of the world's riches countries has to endure. The catastrophic punch that was landed on America, on September 11, 2001 (due to the terrorists attacks) left many in despairing wonder; wonder that developed by an unexpected blow that sidetracked the "land of the free."

Once again the land of the free is in bondage

to chaos resulting September 11th. Thus, do not get strangled by the title of this book. The title holds much more than a means to obtain financial wealth. The title obtains the *voice of God.*

I have found out that God, oftentimes, speaks contrary to our situations. For instance, He told Abram to go to a place unknown so He could bless him. God told Abram, "When you get to that *unknown* land I am going to bless you, and you shall be the father of many nations. I am going to bless your seed innumerably, (paraphrased.)" (These are the instructions God gave Abram, later known as Abraham, see Genesis 12. I also elaborate on this later in the book). This was totally contradictory to Abraham's situation because Abraham's child production seed was dead. He was ninety-nine years old, and past his child producing age. Abraham was in a situation that looked impossible. Are you in a situation that looks impossible? Have you received a word that God would counteract those impossibilities in your life, and miraculously turn them around? Well keep reading!

God has been dispersing words of prosperity to His people in nations that have been in a financial plummet. The message far surpasses the subject of finances, only. God has been showing that He is the only stable thing in life. For so long, we have held our trust in the economic system, in people, and politics. On 9/11 God allowed a situation to happen that sent various messages. The moment calamity fell on the U.S., people connected in an uncommon way. The situation blinded us from hate, dislike, selfishness, and jealousy. People started to rush after God like they had never done before. Everyone from high profile Hollywood stars, to politicians, to rural families found themselves searching for what many call "a higher power," which is God.

It is sad that God allowed a tragic situation to force people to alter their faith, their values, and to press into who He is.

We have allowed our attention to be diverted from the truth. The truth is not in your money, your job, or even yourself. The truth is in "The Provider and Sustainer" of your money, your job, and yourself. We know Him as our "King of Glory!"

You want more?

There is a war going on. This is not some physical war where one country strong- arms another country for control of their goods and/or services. There is a war going on in the invisible, spiritual realm. This war cannot be won by political superiority, or because of economical structure. This is an individual, yet, collective war. It is between God and His enemy. It is also the God in you, or the God that wants to dwell in you versus that which you face. It is a *spiritual* war.

We face battles in life to help build us for spiritual warfare. If we fail to hear the message from our individual battles, the enemy will use the battles we face to keep us separated from God or to separate us from God. For instance, if the enemy can create space between you and God; then he diminishes the space between you and him (the enemy). Therefore, you will find yourself moving *closer* to the enemy and *farther away* from God. As a result, he (the enemy) keeps you from fervently praying and worshiping God.

If your faith is locked into the things in life, as opposed to the God who controls all things, then life will eventually bolster over you. As the nation turned to God for help, God is calling for you to do the same on an individual basis. Turn your faith to Him for help, and give Him your life totally. This is the only way you can survive.

You must deepen your spiritual relationship for the battle you face. Even though the battle is between you and that which *you* face, the best way for survival is for us to survive together. You must realize that my faith in God cannot save you, and your relationship with God depends on you. Nevertheless, there is power in numbers. We are all to be members of one body. You are a key component to the body (see Romans 12). It is an individual battle. Hence, if we take care of our *individual* spiritual business we will make a statement *corporately*. If you fail to accomplish *your* assignment, the remaining body will take a hit. I need you, just as you need me.

For instance, your bodily fingers are designed for a specific use, your feet play a significant role, and your eyes are granted a designated honor. Likewise, you have a fitting position in the body of Christ. It is your job to find out what that role is. You are more significant than you really know.

Though I must fight my own battle, we are a team. I must play my role, just as you must play yours. My task may be to incur vision for the body, while your task may be to provide stability, as the foot. We may be distant from one another, but that does not minimize our importance to the body. We have to learn how to work as a unit. It is virtually impossible for the fingers to do their job if the wrist has been detached from the arm. Thus, you must first learn who you are, and what your purpose is before you can learn the power we have when we function collectively. You don't have to trust in me, because, as the eye, I might go blind. You need to be committed to the centerpiece of the body: the heart. The body has a chance, as long as, the heart is alive and pumping. In the spiritual—the centerpiece of the body is God. He lives eternally. We must commit and trust in Him.

As you continue to read this book, it will enlighten your understanding. This book is a directive for the Christian believer. It is for the rich and poor alike. It is also created for the people of this generation: young and old. The nutrients within this book will help energize you for your daily battles. Thus, it will help those that wonder about the genuine presence of God. A lot of the things in this book are broken down for the sake of those that lack the spiritual inclination necessary to really comprehend what is being said. In order to remain focused in this book, you must have a hunger for what God wants you to know. You must also have a passion for God's Word.

This book will help you find your true fulfillment. It will also help you view yourself as God views you; discover what it takes to reach your destiny; and look inside yourself to gain the strength it takes to overcome your battles. Everything you need to make it in life is in the vicinity of your area. Why waste your money on calling psychics, or other hotlines, when God said you can get the answers you need from Him. Why spend time and money playing the lotteries, and on moneymaking gimmicks if money is not the answer for mending your life? Discover what you really need. I charge you to read "Wealthy in a Poverty Estate." You may find out that your answers to success are closer than you ever thought. Please have enough faith to flip open, and read page by page.

How to Read Wealthy in a Poverty Estate Chapter Ending Principles

Everyday for at least seven days, repeat the Scriptures at the end of the chapters. These Scriptures are a part of what should be practical principles assisting your growth with God. Repeat these Scriptures while you are at home, the mall, or on the job. Get these Scriptures down into your spirit. There is also a small prayer designed for you to say after you read the practical principles. As a practice, let's try one for the end of this preface.

Practical Principles
Romans 10:9

"That if thou shalt confess with thy mouth the Lord Jesus, and shalt believe in thine heart that God hath raised him from the dead thou shalt be saved."

There is no other way to be saved without following the guidelines of this scripture. All God asks you to do is to make a truthful confession with your mouth that Jesus is Lord, and to believe that God raised Jesus from the dead. That's all! Do you believe it? If you died tonight where would you go?

I don't ask you to repeat this Scripture everyday for seven days, unless you have not accepted it totally. Once you follow the Scripture's instructions, and you believe what you have done regarding the scripture, then you are free to move forward. I want you to know that God says you are saved once you follow these instructions.

After you have proclaimed this scripture, the first step to becoming a new person is taking place already in the invisible. Though you cannot *see* your transformation, do not think it is not happening. God loves you enough to save you from hell, despite the mistakes you have made, even if you were to die tonight! All you have to do is follow the scriptural guidelines above. You will reap many benefits!

Chapter 1

The Beginnings

Led By Leadership

Through the guidance of an active God who is definitely an active spirit, comes the reason for this literary work. Though mentally absent as to *why* God has placed such a mandate on me for this composite; I must write. Such ignorance of God's reason stimulates questions that beg to ask, "Why!" Why would He choose me to write a book? After all, I have invested a vast amount of time sharpening other talents.

Have you ever felt like God was taking you away from your dominant talents only to find out you have *other* talents He desired to use?

I believed God would use me to touch people through other talents I possess. Certainly writing a book never crossed my mind as a talent, especially on something I know nothing about! Or do I? Baffled by compounding questions that demand answers, I can only trust and obey "My Mighty Counselor!" So how do I begin?

Let's Pray!

Father we glorify you. Not because of what you can do or have done, but because you are God. You have chosen us before the foundations of the world. You understood what we would become in life before life itself understood us. Yet life doesn't understand us, but it understands the God in us and the God that desires to dwell in others. You knew exactly what it would take to gravitate toward you. You allowed pain, destruction, loss, confusion, anger, persecution, and many other afflictions to draw us closer; as if there was even a slight possibility it would not work. You knew it would work. You said you would never leave us nor forsake us. You said you would not put more on us than we could bear. So, we cast our burdens on you believing you will continue to sustain and disallow the righteous to be moved. I petition that you abide within, and guide me without, as I write. Allow the words that illuminate these pages to LEAP OUT at the purposed reader. Feed your flock; cause them to be saved and set free, and to develop a drive for a closer relationship with you. Oh, God, deplete doubt and enrich faith. In Jesus name, Amen!

In writing "the beginnings" of this book, I believe God has posed my spirit to assume the position fit to help nourish the seed(s) you obtain. Through the course of this writing I clasp hands with you as my reader, leading a journey through different phases of my life. Each phase I have gone through, or am currently going through—phases that will help both of us better assess life's dysfunctions. Other things will be integrated as the Holy Spirit guides me.

Alpha

This February 13, 2003 (the day this book was started), we happened to be in a financial crisis alert. We are in a period where job security has become secure enough for the day at hand. This is a period where financial freedom seems liberal only for food, shelter, and gas, where war is at hand, and life triggers an emotional roller coaster. People are trying to sustain their finances for the cause at hand. People are losing jobs that once seemed more secure than the foundation of concrete. In the midst of laborious work efforts, we have failed to realize that even concrete cracks.

I have heard that a crisis as such, generally does not hurt the rich or well off. The true reality is, even the extremely wealthy encounter problems that reveal themselves as a daily crisis. Whether it is for our individual enjoyment or family fulfillment, we apply our efforts toward particular arenas to reap the joys of life. Oftentimes, our focus becomes drowned in those arenas until we loose grips with other things of equal or of more importance.

While I am unsure about this book, others are unsure about what lies ahead. My blur seems but a raindrop falling from the sky compared to the thunderstorm of others' worries.

The Capacity to Understand

For the sake of readers who may find themselves lost during the reading, when I say the word "life" I am generally summing up everything we deal with in life. *"In the beginning God created the heaven and the earth (Genesis 1:1)."* Before anything was manifested, we find the beginning of all things predicated on God. Throughout Genesis 1 we witness the fact that everything appears after "God called," or "God said." God *voiced* life to exist and life obeyed. *"And he is before all things, and by him all things consist" (Colossians 1:17)*. Therefore, life is subject unto God. Nothing in life precedes God. If nothing precedes God, obviously, God is the head and in charge. Now that we have established *who* is in charge let's discuss life.

Understanding life is as impossible as Goliath defeating David without the voice of the Lord (Goliath did not defeat David—David was one of God's chosen men who defeated Goliath through his faith in God). We will never be able to totally understand life, or the see life in a clear picture. Life often paints for us a blurred picture. It will totally ground us trying to focus the lens on life. Understanding life or rather, the things we deal with in life is impossible.

As a 25 year old, I do not understand the waves of life we must battle to make it back to shore. While we are floating in the midst of the clear blue ocean, with the sun smiling down on our smooth silky skin, with the changing of a second, a gray cloud appears. The cloud at hand takes over the sky in its entirety, begins to pour rain, while the winds arise, flips our float, and sends us gasping for air crying, "Help!"

Life is very much symbolic. Life will eventually flip our float and leave us gasping for air in the midst of a raging storm. Life yields for no man nor woman, no beast nor bird, the poor nor rich. It doesn't matter the skin pigmentation, age, or station in life—life consists of changes through seasons.

Once we understand that life is comprised of *seasons,* it will give us a better assessment of life. As we begin to understand the seasons of life, our life-filled understanding will help us comprehend God better. We must conclude God is in control. God controls all—from sunrise to the sun awakening. The fact that He is in control brings about comfort.

For instance, it's a dark cold winter night with no one around but you and a companion. You are lying down in the bedroom watching a very intriguing movie, eating popcorn, and drinking a coke. Your companion is stationed in another room. The movie has encapsulated your attention, so much so that it causes you to ignore everything else surrounding you. As time passes, you notice that it is very windy outside. Immediately, the tree outside your window slams into the house because of the boisterous winds. The electricity shuts off in the entire house. The house is in total blackout. You become frantic, anxious, and not to mention confused with what has recently happened.

One second everything is smooth sailing; then, with the transformation of another second, everything seems to appear in a downward motion. Your companion shouts your name to insure you are okay. They reiterate their expertise with power outages and electrical problems; so you are not to panic. They tell you they are going outside to check the electrical wiring and the fuse box . . .

By knowing someone is in the circumstance with you, and the fact that they are experienced enough to change the outcome, gives you comfort. You now begin to understand that, in time, things should be okay. As a result, what has happened becomes subject to your companion's expertise. They have the authority to apply their strengths (expertise with electrical problems) to what has become weak (electricity shut out in your house). Your companion now assumes responsibility for controlling the situation.

God is much the same. He wants to assume responsibility for whatever we are dealing with. He desires that we trust and depend on His expertise during the situation. Every storm holds a promise; stipulating the promise is a rainbow. God has promised that no matter how raging the storm becomes, He will not allow total destruction. The simplicity of that statement tells us we are not in the storm alone. It tells us He has the authority to call a peace treaty. It also connotes that though our understanding with life is unfruitful, life understands who is in control. Once we understand the *Author,* we can understand the *Finisher.* Everything in between the beginning and the end is used to sculpt a fine creation.

Transformation

About three years ago, I encountered a dramatic experience with God. I was a collegiate bas-

ketball player in my junior year. We were returning home from a road game when a teammate and I
began discussing afflictions we faced. In the midst of
the conversation, I noticed there was pain he bottled
up within himself, because tears soon fell down his
cheeks. As I witnessed his frustrations, his external
release was so efficacious it punctured my heart. I,
too, began to weep. Of course it was pitch dark so
those that were still awake could not see what was
going on. The rest of the team were asleep.

We finally arrived back on campus. Everyone
was awake and ignited talk about going to a party. I
had come to the point where partying was no longer a
part of my lifestyle. I told them I would not make the
trip. I had a roommate at the time, and he went with
the others to party. I made it back to my dorm room.
The clock spoke 12:00 A.M. Our beds were kept par-
allel from each other: his bed on the east wall and my
bed adjacent to the west wall. It was our practice to
surround the threshold with towels, so that no light
could peep through the door. Our room was kept
pitch dark.

I freshened up, turned on my stereo, put my
gospel compact disc in, and switched the CD to
track number six entitled, "It shall be done!" I got
in my bed with my head at the foot post, and went
to sleep.

I woke up in the middle of the night. The upper
proportion of my body literally arose off my bed. My
body began to shake like a mother shaking an orange
juice carton for her sibling. I turned my head to look

at the clock. The clock was positioned on top of the shelf above the stereo. The clock was now reflecting 2:30 A.M. The same song was playing (the stereo may have been on repeat), and I noticed that I could see everything throughout our room. It was as if a light was shining so bright it illuminated the entire room: mind you we kept the room pitch dark. I looked over at my roommate's bed. I remember thinking, "He probably thinks I am going crazy!" To my surprise his bed was still made, so I knew he had not made it in. This was by far an act of God. The Holy Spirit gently let my body down. This was one of the most amazing feelings I had ever experienced. It was so amazing a smile took authority over my face. I started shaking "self-willed" trying to grasp the same feeling. To my avail the response was nonproductive.

About a week later, I heard the voice of God with great clarity. He said, "You shall be prosperous all the days of your life!" I immediately conveyed God's promise for prosperity to mean mere money. I thought, "Man, I'm bout to be ri-i-ich!" For the first time I heard God speak with a full assurance of whose voice it was. I must emphasize assurance, because beforehand I was somewhat skeptical of God speaking. I was skeptical, particularly, because I did not have a personal experience with hearing God speak. I always heard people say God still speaks, but I never witnessed it until this situation took place. For about the next two years after hearing what God spoke to me, I did not go without money. (Note, God's prosperity means more than only money, however, during this time I didn't realize it). From that day until a few months after I graduated, I always had and never lacked.

After graduating, I moved to Dallas with my uncle. After months of searching for a job, I finally got an interview. I had a morning appointment, but never made the interview. I looked for the area where the job interview was held, but never found the actual place. I finally turned around and headed back home. About five miles from home I heard a continuous extremely loud noise coming from my car. I said to myself, *"I do not have anyone's money to fix nobody's car."*

I stopped at a local Goodyear autocare. They drove my vehicle into the car bay to do a diagnostic check. The erroneous noise was coming from my brakes. My brakes were damaged. My rear rotors were warped, my cylinders were heavily leaking, and my pads were rubbing metal to metal. The estimated price to fix the problem was $450 dollars. The cost to repair my rear brakes alone was a little over half that amount. I had my last $160 dollars in my pocket. I went to the glove compartment to get a bag of quarters I had been saving. I counted all the quarters, which was a little over $40 dollars. The manager and I began adding the money, which eventually fell short of the required amount. He reduced the cost to the amount that I had, and authorized the workers to repair my rear brakes since they were the worst.

While my brakes were being repaired, a conversation arose between the manager and me. Over the course of our conversation, we began talking about God. We had a long interesting conversation. After a couple of hours, the technician brought my work order to the manager to be finalized. The tech said my brakes were about out and he could not understand why I never heard the noise until that particular moment. I also took a look at the brakes before they fixed them, and everything they said was valid.

As the manager was printing my check-out ticket, he mentioned he had to find one more worker to help him work the front desk. He was not implying anything; he was only holding a general conversation. In fact, he did not know my situation of being jobless. I took the opportunity to ask him why he was still looking to hire someone when I was in his face. To make a long story short he hired me on the spot. God knew my situation, and what looked like a minor set back, tuned out to be a current gain. God turned what looked bad, and used it for good (Genesis 50:20).

Believing What Can't be Seen

After working at Goodyear for almost a year, I had an opportunity to move to Washington D.C./ Maryland area. Faith in a dream led me to the state of Maryland.

Everything was set to flow smoothly before I departed from Dallas to go to D.C./Maryland. My house was situated, my job looked secure, and my future looked bright. Days before my departure, everything that looked ordered was now shaken. I did not know where I would stay or even if my job remained stable. I prayed about it and found a calming peace. I decided to trust in God and be led by His peace (Colossians 3:15).

Driving from Texas to D.C./Maryland without precisely knowing what was in store seemed okay. The drive took me through the remainder of Texas, Arkansas, Tennessee, Virginia, then to D.C. While going through Virginia it dawned on me that I really did not have a place to stay. I was somewhere from 12 to 16 hours into the journey to D.C./Maryland, and suddenly the thought hit me. I was extremely optimistic toward things working out preceding the trip; everything negative was overlooked. I refused to deal with reality. Tears began to pour down my face. I had become frantic over this situation. Seconds later I heard God say "I got a place for you to stay." My tears immediately dried, and I was overcome by an unusual joy once I heard God speak those words. Once again I gained resolution about the situation, and continued my journey. I finally got to D.C./Maryland. My housing was bleak, job was shaky, but I still believe God was holding my future.

My first night in D.C./Maryland was dramatic. My home had become my truck. I feasted on my tears and the pain felt from a discouraging circumstance. I remember saying to God "I thought you had a place for me to stay. I guess sleeping in my truck is it, huh? Well, I won't complain." I finally cried myself to sleep.

For the first couple of days in Maryland, I

knew I had to manage the little money that I had left, I would park at a hotel late at night to savor what I had. As scared as I was each day and night, on the hotel parking lot is where I would sleep. In the mornings, I went inside the hotel to eat continental breakfast, brush my teeth in the public restroom, and then I left to go to a local facility I found while sight seeing. There I purchased a membership for $40/month, which allowed me a place to stay fit and remain cleaned up. I did not know how long I would have to stay out of my vehicle, but I did realize that I did not have another $40 to pay for another month of membership. All I had was my faith that I would quickly find a job, and things would get better real soon. Gratefully, I knew one person in the area. I decided to call him to come workout with me. I went to pick him up, so we could work out together. Trailing the workout he popped the big question, "YO, DEE WHERE ARE YOU STAYING?" To his unbelief I responded with "in my car!" He was staying home with his parents. They were also accommodating his sisters, his girlfriend, and one of his friends who was in the area finishing her law degree. I was not accepting an invitation to preoccupy unavailable space. I cut the conversation short so I could get washed up and get him back home.

As I was taking a shower, a mysterious feeling overtook me that resembled something special was happening. I got dressed and ready to go. As I was approaching my friend, he was sitting on a bench talking to this older guy. The guy looked to be in his late

40's. The man switched from the conversation they were having. He told my friend he had open space if he (my friend) ever had anyone else that needed a place to stay. I assume this man presented such an invitation due to the few people that he knew had come to the area that my friend's parents previously accommodated. I don't think he wanted my friend to put anymore pressure on his parents by asking them to accommodate another person. My friend began to smile and pointed up at me. The man looked startled and asked what was going on.

I sat down and gave him the basics of my situation. We talked about it for a very small amount of time, then our conversation somehow switched to discussing God. Next, he told me he had a house built up from the ground with rooms he was not using. He told me that he and his wife, along with his son, and daughter were occupying the home. His invitation was extended to me to occupy one of the vacant rooms if I so desired. To shorten the story, I met his family that night, and moved in. I discovered that they are a Christian family. My stay there was astounding; it was as if we had known each other for years. They accepted me as one of their own, and we remain extremely close to this day. I am still mesmerized by the fact they took a stranger in on the first day of their encounter. You must understand the area in which they reside has an extremely high crime rate, and we are talking about a *stranger* moving in. They took me in upon first encounter, and they did it with seemingly no worries. God told me this revelation in Virginia. It was definitely divine intervention.

As time flowed, I finally moved back to Dallas, Texas. I moved back with my uncle until I could get things stable enough to get my own place. I got a job at a place called J.C. Penney Corporate through a temp agency. I worked in the marketing/ advertising department. My paycheck was fair, but my liabilities (bills) overwhelmed my assets, so my income never communed with my wallet. I held this job for about four months: this being the fulfillment of my temp assignment. I figured through high praises, from my supervisor and co-workers, I would have been made a permanent employee once my assignment was complete. It did not happen. I found myself back at square one; having to find another job.

I tried to gain some stability, but it seemed like stability would never happen. The closer I believed I was getting to God, the more I went without. The stronger the struggle; the deeper the pain. I could not understand how one could be so faithful to God while trying to live life productively; could be going through so much confusion. I found myself in a position that was foreign—living off a credit card. My gas, my food, and my limited shopping for necessities were all purchased on credit. Living on credit was more than a choice; it was a must. Whenever my friends would invite me to a place, I would come up with some lame alternative for not going. My finances totally hindered me from having fun if the fun required money.

"So God tells me I'm going to be prosperous all the days of my life, huh. Why have my finances become a hindrance to me? What do I do now? How can I live as an exemplary for anyone being in this type of condition? No money, buying food becomes harsh, job dissatisfaction, car repair at hand, cannot afford to hang out with my friends; what next?" I thought I had encountered enough trouble through prior stages of my life. Once God gave me a promise, I found myself fighting to obtain that promise. Just to simply remain strong enough to live right for God was a battle for me.

Practical Principles
II Corinthians 5:7
"For we walk by faith, not by sight . . ."

As we can see by swimming our way through Chapter 1, this Scripture was key in helping me overcome what I was facing at the time. I had to believe the things God said to me if I wanted to make it through the battle. My faith had to activate into . . .

the promise of God telling me I would be prosperous all my days, even when I *lost* everything

the promise of God telling me I had a place to stay even when the natural facts told me I did *not* have a place to stay

Walking by faith and not what I could see physically, helped me to overcome my battles. It is a lot better to look at things with a spiritual sense, as opposed to, seeing the chaos and worrying about what *you* can do to change them. Sometimes trying to do things yourself is not the right answer. When you seek God, and rely on Him you will always come out on top. It may take a little time, but you will be victorious.

Proverbs 3:5

"Trust in the LORD with all thine heart, and lean not unto thine own understanding."

Though our situations may look lopsided, we must believe that God will see us through it. This is why our relationship with God is extremely important. It is important because God will show us the map that will help lead us into the stage of deliverance. If we trust in God, we will eventually find ourselves graduating from the problems that disturb us. If we constantly focus on our problems instead of enjoying the day God has granted us, our problems will make our days seem like they are never going to end. No one wants to live everyday of their life in days that never seem to end when things are not going right. We must trust in God, and rely not on the current view of our situation. We must grab hold to the promise that God has given us and He will see us through it. If you cannot think of any promises God has given you, here is one from Proverbs 3:6, *"In all thy ways acknowledge him (God), and he (God) shall direct thy (your) path."*

Summary Prayer

God, I ask for forgiveness for not trusting you with my all. Help me deepen my faith in You and Your words of wisdom. I believe that You are able to do whatever You desire to do. Thank you for caring so much for me. I will not worry about _____ (whatever it is that bothers you) any longer. Help me to walk by faith and not to focus so much on the situation. While I walk by faith, persuade me that everything will be okay; help me understand that You have everything under control.

Chapter 2

Covenant Keeper

One of the promises God gave me was that I would be prosperous all the days of my life. Not long after receiving the promise, I found myself in a struggle contradicting the promise. In this particular case, the promise was predicated on prosperity. Let's dissect the word *prosperity* a little.

Prosperity, the way we normally depict it, deals with a component of economic or financial status. Just as I previously told you, I singled God's promise out to mean prosperity related to a financial basis. "He promised me prosperity!" I shouted, "I am about to be rich!" I believed I was going to receive an influx of money.

To define prosperity by only a means of financial or economic status is an error. This status of prosperity is only a component. It is considered one of the benefits contained within the gift of prosperity. It is much like feasting on a can of mixed fruit. In a can of mixed fruit a person has the opportunity to feast on a variety of different fruit. Once they leave the supplier (for this illustration lets say, the store) with the can, they now have a can containing different facets of the fruit group. They have cherries, pears, peaches, grapes, and pineapples all in one can. Each fruit has a different look and taste. They can even use them for different things. The cherry can be used to top an ice cream sundae, peaches to make peach cobbler, grapes to make grape jelly, pineapples to add flavor to ham, and the pear to make a nutritious smoothie. Inside the can there is more than just cherries, or just pears, or just peaches; it is a can of *mixed* fruit. With God, prosperity is the same. Prosperity is not just money. It is composed of many different facets: each face of prosperity with a different taste and use.

Faces

I have found that in the Old Testament, prosperity is used several ways. Let's dissect three of them:

First, is the *peace of prosperity.* In the Hebrew language peace is translated as the word *Shalowm* or *Shalom.* This is a prosperity that resembles completeness, tranquility, or a peaceful estate. This is the name added to Jehovah (an admonishing name for God-similar to a nickname), as when Gideon had an encounter with God in Judges 6. In this chapter, God chose a man named Gideon to deliver Israel out of the hands of the Midianites. The Midianites had become an enemy to the children of Israel. While Gideon was under a tree separating wheat, he met an angel of God. The angel notified Gideon that God chose him to lead Israel into deliverance from the Midianites.

Gideon wanted a sign that signified what the angel told him was, definitely, a word from God. Gideon told the angel he was going to prepare a meal offering, and he would bring it back for God to perform a sign that would confirm what the angel told him was true. Gideon prepared a baby goat, and some bread as the offering. When Gideon returned, the angel touched the flesh (baby goat) and unleavened cakes (bread), and fire arose out of the rock. Stemming from this dramatic experience, Gideon realized he had seen an angel face to face. God then intervened and told Gideon *"Peace be unto thee; fear not: thou shalt not die."* Later, Gideon built an altar and called it Jehovah Shalom (Judges 6:24), or the God of peace.

In the book of Psalms we find different passages such as Psalms 30:6, which denote this facet of prosperity. In Chapter 30 we find the psalmist encountering a stage of deliverance. The psalmist starts off through stages of thanksgiving, praise, and worship. In verse six he says, *"And in my prosperity I said, I shall never be moved."* This version of prosperity derives from the Hebrew word *Shalom*.

If we view the passage with one of the substitutes—one way to read it would be as thus, "And in my {peace} I said, I shall never be moved." In reading the passage as such, we find a servant through his spiritual understanding paying reverence to God.

He acknowledges God for His limitless mercy and matchless authority to deliver a bound soul from a troubling situation. Allow me to explain. In Verse 5, the psalmist declares, *That weeping may endure for a night, but joy cometh in the morning.* He then conjugates verse 6. As a result of his deliverance from an anguishing situation, he is embellished in a calmness that locks him into a place of assurance. He was locked into an assurance—that rest in a never-forsaking God.

Many of us can relate to this situation. We have been in disastrous storms that seemed like the day would never brighten. After being soaked by hail size raindrops for so long, to witness 'just' a glimpse of sunlight fight its way through a struggle with a selfish cloud, is liberating. When the storm ceases and the day breaks forth, it paves the way to unlock our bound-up soul from a cell of corruption. To keep faith that one day we will see the chief officer unlock our door to deliverance, instead of pass our cell to unlock a cellmate's, is refreshing. It humbles us, draws a thankful spirit, and it brings a spirit of peace to know that we have enough faith to believe one day we will make it out of the storm. Whenever that day comes, we will then understand that our faith was rewarded. It boosts our confidence to see that God cared enough for us to show us mercy.

To understand God as our shield, our buckler, and our peace that grants us peace—gives us the audacity to say, *And in my {prosperity, peace, tranquility} I said, I shall never be moved (Psalms 30:6).*

When we experience the peace of God in any situation, we know that His peace will seemingly numb us; almost blind us to everything that tried to deter our focus. As a result, we have been taught about the God of peace while walking in the peace of God. If you have never experienced it, then I have just told you—the "God of peace" means God has the authority to give us peace. It also means we must seek Him for His goods; in this case His peace.

The only way we can get canned fruit is by purchasing the fruit from the supplier. We have to go to the store to get the goods we desire. Just as the store furnishes the canned goods, God furnishes peace. The peace of God means that peace is a derivative of God. It is birthed from God. It comes from God. When we find freedom from a distraught situation, we often walk in the peace of God. We acknowledge that God is the author of that peace; or that He is the God of the peace that we walk in.

The following are two promises that will help us better gauge this first face of prosperity:

The *first* one is, *"Let your conversation be without covetousness: and be content with such things as ye have: for he hath said, I WILL NEVER LEAVE THEE, NOR FORSAKE THEE (Hebrew 13:5)."*

The *second* one is, *"Cast thy burden upon the LORD, and he shall sustain thee: he shall never suffer the righteous to be moved (Psalms 55:22)."*

Here we discover two concrete promises:

The first one is that He has promised not to leave us alone. The second promise comes as a result of giving him our cares and burdens. God says He will never suffer the righteous (us) to be moved. The first thing we must get into our spirit is that God promises He will never leave us desolate (alone). He knows our situations. He is *around* our situations, He is *in* our situations, and *above* our situations. We must get this embedded in the roots of our soul. Once we understand that God is with us, it will open the door for Him to comfort us while we are in the battle. If we know that we are not fighting alone, then we know we have a partner to discuss strategies with, and to confide in.

Psalms 55:22 is the key scripture in helping understand Psalms 30:6. Here is the key; *"Cast thy burden upon the Lord,"* or trust the Lord with whatever cares we have . . .give our cares to Him and let Him deal with them. How do we give our cares/burdens to God? Through the dialogue of prayer! *"Be careful for nothing; but in every thing by prayer and supplication with thanksgiving let your request be made known unto God. And the peace of god, which passeth all understanding, shall keep your hearts and minds through Christ Jesus (Philippians 4:6,7)."*

Communicate with God about the problem as if you were talking to your dad in the natural: *"God I give this situation over to you. I understand you are my burden bearer; and you are in fact stronger than I am. The load is too heavy for me to carry, so I hand my problems over to you."*

What should your request be? *"Lord sustain me, give me strength, help me endure, deliver me .*

. . ." Be honest with what you need God to do. The servant then says with thanksgiving, *"Lord I thank you for caring enough to take the task of bearing my burdens, and releasing me from the task."*

Then the scripture says, *"And the peace of God, which passeth all understanding. . . ."* AH HA! *This is the exact peace that enabled the psalmist to say in Psalms "And in my prosperity I said, I shall never be moved (Psalms 30:6)."* Or in other words, "Through hell and high water God has granted me His incomprehensible peace by which I believe no calamity of this world can faze me."

The second use of the word prosperity derives from the Hebrew word *tsalech.*

Tsalech in Hebrew means to rush, advance, be expedient, make progress. Wouldn't you love to witness our God of grace pause rush hour traffic (everyone trying to get to Him) to attend to your damaged cry? This is exactly what David was petitioning God for in Psalms 118:25. Here we find the same word (prosperity) preoccupying David's cry, but now in a much different use. He laments *"Save now, I beseech thee, O LORD: O LORD, I beseech thee, send now prosperity (Psalms 118:25)."* This chapter begins by charging the audience to give thanks to a merciful God. The writer understands who delivered him and his peers, when they faced troubling situations. So he commands the recipients of God's mercy to pay tribute to Him (God) who "showed them mercy."

When I was growing up one of my uncles would bully me. He would twist my arm and pull it behind my back. The higher he elevated my arm behind my back, the more intense the pain was. I tried to act so strong and composed; I would not give in to him. He would tell me "Say mercy, say mercy." I replied, "Man, I ain't givin' in!" After minutes of this process, he would immediately over indulge my arm to the top of my back. I would shout "HAVE MERCY!" Sometimes he would wait until I got teary eyed and let me go. Other times I noticed my Grandfather would rush into the room, and my uncle would immediately release me.

My uncle understood who was in charge, and my grandfather's presence alone acknowledged his authority. Granddaddy did not have to say nothing, nor do anything. Regardless of the fact that my uncle is his direct son, Granddaddy still accepted me as his child. Therefore he would not tolerate anyone disrespecting his children: whether it was his children hurting his children, or someone outside his family hurting his children. His basis was—do not hurt any of my children.

Granddaddy would rush in to save me from a troubling situation. This was just what I needed. I needed a higher authority to rush in and grant me peace. After a few times of going through this with my uncle, I realized all I had to do in this situation was shout granddaddy's name and he would rush in. Sometimes, I would shout about other issues when I really did not need him. He would not show up. At first, I could not understand why he would not come help me. I learned that when you are in real trouble;

when you really need help, your shout has a different tone. There is something about a "merciful shout!" David had a merciful shout.

David had been through enough battles to know that it could not have been anyone but God who delivered him. How about David killing a nine feet tall giant named Goliath with a stone? While everyone else was wallowing in the fear of being destroyed by this giant; David declared, *"Who is this uncircumcised Philistine, that he should defy the armies of the living God (I Samuel 17:26)?"* Or what about his encounter with the king of Israel named Saul who was vehemently trying to kill him (David) (I Samuel 30)? David found himself constantly flee-ing from his closest companion's father. His clos-est companion was Jonathan, Saul's son. David had great respect for the king, and more for God, that he would not defend himself against the king.

How would you feel if you had to watch your front and your back because of the enemy's hot pur-suit? Everywhere David turned, Saul had his men hunting for him. David went through enough to understand God as his deliverer. David also under-stood that once you go through a heated battle, when God delivers you; His (God's) peace will prevail. Therefore, David shouted for mercy; God's imme-diate deliverance, to calm what were his current storms.

When we are going through a discombobulated situation it is easy to become frustrated. Oftentimes, we began to wonder and doubt. Whenever the situation is finally resolved, we gain a peace about the situation.

This is the prosperity David requested in Psalms 118. He says LORD I need you to rush in like a raging flood. Just as the presence of my Grand-daddy ceased the immediate action of my uncle, God's presence will cause demons to flee. David had a spiritual understanding of this. He voices it, "Save now, I beseech thee, O LORD: O LORD, I beseech thee, SEND NOW PROSPERITY. Rush in now, I need you now, have mercy."

Over the course of reading Psalms 118, we can see David was dealing with some physical battles. In verse six he says *"The Lord is on my side; I will not fear: what can man do unto me?"* In verse eight he declares, *"It is better to trust in the Lord than to put confidence in man."* He talks about destroying his enemies in the name of the Lord. So I ask you, "Why would David ask God for some *money* to help accomplish this task!" Money could not resolve this problem. David was asking for some immediate *deliverance.*

A third way the word prosperity is used in the Old Testament evolves from the Hebrew word *Towb* {tobe}. The word in its use means, good. In Zecha-riah 1:17 God is speaking to His prophet Zechariah regarding the Israelites. God begins the conversation with the prophet Zechariah discussing displeasures with Zechariah's forefathers, and His (God's) peo-ple. Zechariah later describes different visions and dreams he had. In discussing his dreams with God

and the angel of God, Zechariah learned of the indignation God had toward Jerusalem and the cities of
Judah. God was angry with His people for not taking
heed to His request. God told them to turn away from
their sins and wicked ways. They failed to do so, and
fell subject to God's anger for their disobedience.

The Bible says the angel of the LORD asked
God, "How long would He (God) withhold His
mercy from Jerusalem, and from the cities of Judah?"
(God was indignant toward Jerusalem because they
refused to repent of their evil ways and acts; things
from which He had previously instructed them to
turn away). Zechariah says God's reply was good
and comfortable.

Zechariah said the angel told him what was in
God's heart toward Jerusalem, the city of Zion, and the
heathen that helped forward the affliction. In return,
God spoke to Zechariah of His plan to re-establish
His presence, mercy, and house amongst Jerusalem.
In one of the dreams, Zechariah talked about four
horns that scattered Judah—a horn in the Bible rep-
resents strength. The *four horns* were *four leaders*
that use their strengths to scatter God's people. They
built idol gods to lead the Israelites astray and the
Israelites were committing idolatry. As a result, the
Israelites place of worship was bashed (destroyed).
The city of Jerusalem was also demolished. If the
Israelites had listened to God this never would have
happened. Later, God had enough compassion to
rebuild the city, and to re-establish His people.

God told the prophet His plan to dwell in the

midst of Jerusalem and surround the city as a "wall of fire." The Lord spoke of a turn around for the nations that spoiled (or oppressed) God's people. He told the prophet that He would "shake His hand, and those that spoiled the servants would become spoil to the servants." (The Lord's hand signifies power.) God also spoke of a gravitational pull of the nations toward the Holy city of Jerusalem. God talked about His passionate love for His people. In relation, He said He would re-build and re-establish the broken temple in the city.

God told the prophet something vital in the turn around during His explanation to Zechariah as to what happened, and what was about to happen. In Zechariah 1:17 Zechariah said, *"Cry yet, saying, Thus saith the LORD of hosts; My cities through **prosperity** shall yet be spread abroad; and the LORD shall yet comfort Zion, and shall yet choose Jerusalem."* God gave instructions to Zechariah as to what he (Zechariah) was to do and to say involving His people, and Jerusalem. He told Zechariah that His (God's) cities, through prosperity, shall yet be spread abroad. Understanding the word prosperity in its use here, is more comprehensive, once we look at what happened to the same cities.

As we bounce back to the dream Zechariah had about the four horns, Zechariah said he asked the angel what the horns represented. The angel told Zechariah the four horns were those that "scattered the tribe of God." The same cities that were scattered are the same cities that would be spread abroad. The spread will come about because of God's glory in the holy city. The nations would draw towards the heat and God's wave of glory.

The scenario helps us make a better assessment of the use of the word, prosperity here. We found out the cities were, originally, scattered—which is an irregular distribution—to scatter is a type of division.

I recall being in the midst of different community gatherings, such as, the state fair. While attending the festival, from time to time something distraught would happen. Over the course of time, an argument would take place between two people who developed a disagreement about something. Wanting to see a fight, many people surrounded the two guys. One guy would reveal some sort of weapon: many times a knife or a gun. Someone would see the weapon, and they would shout, "He's got a gun." Everyone would immediately scatter, and vacate the premises. No one really cared *where* they were running or where their run ended. All we knew was to run. As a result of a bad situation, everyone scattered into different areas. Everyone *divided,* one from another, with no direct place to go. This gives us a better assessment of what is means "to scatter."

God told the prophet through prosperity He was going to spread abroad His cities. To spread means to *cover,* to *grow in length or breadth.* The word, *abroad* is defined as, " . . .over a wide area or to exceed the boundaries." In verse 16, God talks about a line being stretched forth over Jerusalem.

Later in chapter 2, Zechariah speaks about a man with a measuring line in his hand. Zechariah said the man with the measuring line said he was measuring the breadth and length of Jerusalem. Once again, to spread means to cover, to grow in length or breadth.

In understanding that God is a God of abundance, it is safe to assess what God is about to do in this case. God said He would *re-build* His temple. He said He would re-establish His presence in the cities of Jerusalem. The man with the measuring line was measuring for the re-building process. If a person is about to build something, they measure the area for the foundation of what they are about to build. This is what the man with the measuring line was doing.

God is about to cause nations from all over to gravitate towards the cities. The gravitation would spread so that it would cover the length and breadth. In chapter 2:4, the angel said Jerusalem shall be inhabited as "towns without walls." The spread would not only cover Jerusalem, but, people would raid and fill Jerusalem as if the country never had boundary lines. It would cover the length and breadth of Jerusalem, and overflow Jerusalem's boundary lines. The cities would gravitate for a good reason. So God said, *"Cry yet, saying, Thus saith the LORD of hosts; My cities through [good] shall yet be spread abroad; and the LORD shall yet comfort Zion, and shall yet choose Jerusalem."* How awesome is God!

Sum Total

The previously discussed ways are at least

three ways God's prosperity in a spiritual sense are used to find God's peace, God's mercy, and God's goodness.

So I refer you back to what God told me earlier in the chapter, "You shall be *prosperous* all the days of your life."

Now I understand that my life shall be full of God's mercy, His goodness, and His peace—which are components of the word *prosperity.* These are the intangibles that God wraps inside the gift of prosperity. Among God's intangibles He adds something tangible; finances.

"Wherefore is there a price in the hand of a fool to get wisdom, seeing he hath no heart to it?" (Proverbs 17:16). God could have given me all the money in the world, and it would not have benefited me. It would benefit me nothing without wisdom; how to use it, where to invest it, how to invest it, sow it, how to make it work for me, and not to become its servant. God is concerned less about giving His children a land full of money with mindless sense.

When I was a child, I would ask my grandmother if she had a couple of dollars. She would reply, "Yeah, and [cents] with it, too!" I never really understood what she meant until I got older. What she was really saying was, "Yeah and [sense] with it, too!" The first way made so much sense, it never dawned on me what she was actually saying. She was conveying to me she had money, and the wisdom that is vital in handling money. She was not foolish with handling her money.

The point of concern is not me *receiving* the money. The message capsulated in the statement is a woman exemplifying her wisdom with money. She understood she could not go out and spontaneously purchase foolish items. Aside from that principle, she willingly gave to others. I am not saying you should just give everyone your stuff upon his or her request. What I *am* saying is you cannot close your hand so tight that nothing can escape. If nothing can escape your hand, there is no room for anything to *enter* your hand. If you are too selfish to *give,* then you are too selfish to *receive;* as selfishness *goes* selfishness *comes.*

Through reading one of Jay Snell's books, he said something that is unequivocally true. He said "investments in the law of God are totally contrary to investments in the law of life." *"There is that scattereth, and yet increaseth; and there is that withholdeth more than is meet, but it tendeth to poverty" (Proverb 11:24).* The law as we know teaches us to invest our possessions within our-self in order to increase. The law of God teaches us to give what we have in order to increase.

It is wise to invest within ourselves. Thus, we should not get contained with the gluttony of our stuff that we lose sense of others needs. *"A man that hath friends must show himself friendly" (Proverbs 18:24).* If we want friends we must show ourselves friendly. If we need money we need to freely give the money we have. If no one ever encourages us, we need to encourage others. God works on a giving principle. We must break our self-indulging spirit and learn how to cater to other people. Much like the teaching of my grandmother, we must be open to give towards others needs. We must give without any motives, implications, or stipulations. As we understand the giving principle, we will see God also works on this principle. Walking out this principle will help us walk in God's paths of prosperity: His peace, His mercy, and His goodness.

God Can't Lie

God will always keep His promises. God will keep His promise no matter what it is. The elderly folk put it like this, "If God said it, then that settles it." He is the only one I know who will make sure that what He said is fulfilled. A child's parent may promise something, and forget what they promised their child. It is the constant reminder of the child that keeps the promise fresh on the parent's mind. A person may have a track record for keeping promises, but even they are prone to find themselves in a position where they cannot carry out their promise.

I am reminded of a lady who God placed in my life. She is a saved saint. She was by my side when I didn't have anything, as a part of my support group. We were not together as boyfriend/girlfriend, neither thought to be. She has been just a true friend. I was constantly being misused by other friends and family. I was being persecuted for trying to live righteous. There were people defaming my name, but this lady was one of few who hung in there with me.

One day she persuaded me to get a telephone line turned on. I knew better, but I also know her as an integral woman of God, so I listened to her, because, from the day we met, she never steered me wrong. She told me that I needed a home phone in case someone really needed to get in contact with me. Everything she said was true. The fact was that I did not have any money to keep another phone bill. I had a cell phone, and because of my financial concern, I felt that was all I needed. She said she had it figured out. She calculated her bills for a year that included my phone bill. She was going to pay for my phone bill for a year. She finally persuaded me to accept her offer.

Well, when the second bill came around she did not pay it. The phone company had incurred different connection fees, late fees, and other fees that we did not understand. I never knew this until my phone was about to get cut off. I was not aware of the bills, because they were forwarded to her home. During this time, I assume she had some things come up that set her back financially. She could not keep her promise to pay the phone bill. My phone got cut off. I got a bad mark on my credit report, which is the only bad mark, and her promise to me became void. This is one of the reasons why the psalmist said; *"It is better to trust in the LORD, than to put confidence in man"* (Psalms 118:8).

Man will let you down, even when his intentions are good, however, God will keep His promise *no matter what.* He said, *"So shall my word be that goeth forth out of my mouth: It shall not return unto me void, but it shall accomplish that which I please, and it shall prosper in the thing whereto I sent it" (Isaiah 55:11).* God will keep His promise.

I reiterate the fact that God told me I would be prosperous all the days of my life. I realize that through my downward days, God has showed His face. The lady that has been by my side was an act of God. She was integrated into my life, in part, as a witness to God's promise to me. When things got a little dreary she helped pick up the slack. She was one of the bridges God laid in my life. The enemy would love for us to focus on our problems, and look past the bridges God laid to help carry us over.

You say, "Well, how can a person look past a bridge?" We look past a bridge by complaining about the thunderous rainstorm we are trying to make it through. When we are constantly complaining about our problems, we miss what God provides for us as a bridge. The bridge could be a person, or it could be encouraging words from a person that helps keep us motivated. Whatever the bridge is, God will make sure His paths for His children are prosperous. He has a book filled with promises. He will keep every one of His promises. Psalms 25:10 says, *"All the paths of the LORD are mercy and truth unto such as keep his covenants and his testimonies."*

All of God's paths are filled with mercy and truth. Remember I told you that God's *mercy was a part of His prosperity.* The word truth in Hebrew means reliable, full of divine instruction, or faithfulness. To be able to walk in God's paths that are filled with mercy and truth, is astounding. Now, those are some prosperous paths. If we keep God's covenants, we will find ourselves walking in His paths. God cannot lie. He said it and that settles it!

Practical Principles

Psalms 55:22

"Cast thy burden upon the LORD, and he shall sustain thee: he shall never suffer the righteous to be moved."

Whatever we are dealing with, we must rest our mind from thinking the worse. As we activate our faith in God, give those things that trouble you over to God. Everytime we start to think the worst, counteract those thoughts with positive thoughts. For instance, if we have someone close to us that consistently falls back into drug rehab, and God has given us positive news regarding them; we need to believe what God has told us. Everytime thoughts of them falling into a relapse creeps into our mind, we need to start envisioning them being a success story—a story about one who developed a hatred for drugs. Then thank God for fulfilling His promise to us. We do not have to be moved by our thoughts or problems, mentally or physically. Give those things that weigh us down to God, and watch Him keep us. He will keep us stable both mentally and physically.

Isaiah 26:3

"Thou (God) wilt keep him (you) in perfect

*peace, whose mind is stayed on thee (God)
because he (you) trusteth in thee (God)."*

Think about that for a moment. The prophet
Isaiah said if we keep our mind on God, He (God)
will grant us *perfect peace.* This is the same peace
that was described in chapter two. When something
is of perfection it is without lack, void of brokenness. It is full, and complete. The only thing I knew
of that was perfect is God. Well, God spoke through
His prophet and said He will give us a perfect peace.
I bet you would love to have a peace that covers you;
keeps you from having to constantly worry about
your situation. I am talking about a peace that dif-
fuses you from the drunkenness of life. Give your
battles over to God, lock your faith into Him, and He
promises to grant you His perfect peace.

Summary Prayer

*I give over*_____*(whatever the situation is belongs here) to you. I believe that you have better things in store for me. Grant me your strength to make it through this test. You promised you would not allow me to be moved if I give you what has become a burden to me. Now I release* _____ *(the burden) over to you. Release your peace into my life and increase my faith so that I can be more confident with the decision I know you have made regarding* _____*(the situation).*

Chapter 3

A Balance Beam

"Beloved I wish above all things that thou mayest prosper and be in good health, even as thy soul prospers" (3 John 1:2). True prosperity is a multi-dimensional facet. If you ever saw a diamond under the illumination of the *"sun,"* you probably noticed a lineage of multicolored rays stemming from the diamond with each multicolored ray shining in multiple directions. The rays are conceived through intercourse from the light with the uniquely shaped glass. As we brainstorm the thought of this illustration, we will notice that no area is vacant of a ray.

If we place ourselves center stage, just as the diamond, under the illumination of the *"Son" (Jesus),* we are designed to emit rays likewise. There should be no area of our life in lack; nothing off balance, and no vacant space unfulfilled. There should not be an overload of rays on one side with just a couple of rays on the opposite. *"Being confident of this very thing, that he which hath begun a good work in you will perform it until the day of Jesus Christ" (Philippians*

1:6). God is one of completeness. What He starts He finishes. What He begins He completes. God wants to shine on us until we resemble His shine in every area He has designed for us to occupy.

"Divers weights, and divers measures, both are them are alike abomination to the Lord" (Proverbs 20:10). Here we find God despises things that cause us to be off balance. *"A just weight and balance are the LORD'S: all the weights of the bag are his [work]" (Proverbs 16:11)*. The word "work" in its use here means *concern*. Therefore God is concerned about the load we carry. He is concerned about what is in our bag. Is each weight helping us live a balanced life? Are they causing us to be deceitful or just? Are we dragging in one area more than any other area? What are our motives, if any? God is concerned about us. Proverbs 11:1 incorporates both a false balance and a just weight by saying, *"A false balance is an abomination to the Lord: but a just weight is his delight."* This assists us with understanding III John 1:2.

In III John, verse 2, John tells the audience he not only prays for our prosperity and wellness, physically, but also, spiritually. He links the internal with the external in verse two by use of the word "even!"

We commonly use the word "even," mathematically, to describe numerals of exact variation. For instance, the number one is even to the number one. Or we use "even" when breaking down even numbers as opposed to odd. We find even numbers apt to break down in two equal characters. For example, we can break down number four by two plus two: or the number ten by five plus five. Or if we balance four apples on a balance beam we would put two apples on one side, and two on the other side. I never did like odd numbers when dealing with math. Odd numbers cannot be broken down into two like characters. The number nine has to be broken down by an odd and an even number; like four plus five. Thus, we cannot balance nine lemons. We will have to place four on one side and five on the other. This will promote an unbalanced beam, or a false balance. John uses the term "even" in verse two, illustrating a desire for the intended audience to grow uniformly.

As described in the math illustrations, John petitions for a *balanced* lifestyle. He says I wish above anything else that we "prosper and be in good health, *even* (or leveled) with thy soul's prosperity." God's prosperity promotes balance as a whole. The author writes as if to be prospering externally and not prospering internally is a curse. It is a false balance. It is deceitful, and persuades deceit. So, the writer persuades the audience to continue in growth internally, or spiritually, while they are growing externally.

In Deuteronomy 25:13, Moses elaborates more on divers weights and measures, and just weights. Later in verse 17, Moses talks about Amalek. He tells the Israelites to remember Amalek's actions after the Israelites exoneration from Egypt. During the transition from Egypt to the Promise Land, Amalek smote those that were feeble because he lacked relationship with God. In verse 19, Moses says once the Lord prospers them through deliverance and possessions, "forget not what Amalek did." In other words, Moses says do not forget who increased us as a nation and empowered us to get wealth. Once we get it, we have to keep our trust in *God* and not our "stuff." We cannot get too high-minded that we look down on others. We cannot lose our relationship with God.

God would much rather for us to be blessed enough just to get by, and have a strong relationship with him, than to have an abundance of wealth with a *minimal* spiritual relationship. *"Better is a little with righteousness than great revenues without right" (Proverbs 16:8).* God is less concerned about promoting us on a job, than He is about us being concerned about our relationship with Him.

As discussed earlier in chapter one of this book, "God is head and in charge." He knows *how* to promote and *when* to promote us on our job. He knows how to soften our boss's hard heart toward us. He knows how to recommend us for a job we are unqualified for, according to man's standards, but overqualified for, according to God's standards. He knows how to deliver our children from drug addictions. God knows what it will take to reconcile our broken marriage. God knows! That is why one of the ways we address God, is to refer to Him as an Omniscient God, because He truly knows *all.*

God knows so much, He understands if He released extreme wealth into our life right now, we would transform. Our trust would switch from God to money, which would cause us to fail God. *"He that trusteth in his riches shall fall: but the righteous shall flourish as a branch" (Proverb 11:28).* So He has to teach us humility, perseverance, reliance solely on Him, and patience—all through longsuffering battles. He has to teach us how to rely on Him through need, and how to remain balanced when required. Our past, plus our present, should help us live a balanced life. God wants us to flourish, but He knows He must teach us how to be a good steward through any means necessary. Oftentimes, God will use the pressures in life to help mold us.

Molded Through the Pressures of Life

Why would it be necessary for a millionaire to give someone a million dollars, and that person go buy three $300,000 cars and a $200,000 home? It would be absurd. In spite of how wonderful it would be, or how nice the millionaire presents himself by giving them such a gift; it would not be a good investment on his part. The millionaire has sowed money into a fool. They have bought those luxuries, and they may still lack *integrity.* They might have three beautiful cars, but they may lack *joy.* What good is a lovely home without *love* inside the home? They had a million dollars and within six months, they are broke again with no *peace. Money cannot buy love, joy, peace, longsuffering, gentleness, goodness, faith, meekness, or temperance.* These are God-granted intangibles called the "fruit of the spirit." These intangibles come through relationship with God. They come through enduring hardship, hard times, growing pains, and maturation. The endurance to conquer comes through our walk with God.

Before walking with God, it probably seemed like you were in control of your own destiny. You really did not have to depend on anyone. You did what you wanted to do, how you wanted to do it. Then you walked through invisible doors of salvation, where everything in your life changed. You were told do(s) and don't(s)—people saying you can do this, but you must separate from that. Someone whispers to you:

-You are not your own, you belong to God.
-God does not like you doing that.
-You cannot live for God, and still flow according to the course of the world.
-You must be separate from the world.
-You found yourself in an unwelcome position.

You may have never agreed to step over the fence if you knew this was what Christianity was all about. As you get closer to God, life pressures you to let go of your relationship with Him.

Maybe you find yourself battling to survive each day with less and less money?

As each day rises and each night falls, your money constantly dissipates. It disintegrates, like a child blowing on the head of a white dandelion. So what do you do when your liabilities swallow your assets whole?

Maybe your confidence has slipped loose like

a child losing foot traction on icy pavements. How do you believe positively when things are quickly falling?

You are fighting a battle where you find yourself having to believe that God can make a difference; that someway, somehow He can change the circumstance. Whereas, before you walked through the doors to salvation, you were never in such vulnerability. The vulnerability coincides with the fact you must now rely on someone other than yourself to remain secure. Oh, yes, you are vulnerable!

You are as vulnerable as a new converted Abram who had to believe God would sustain him. Abram had to believe that God would hold to His (God's) end of the promise once he (Abram) moved on God's voice to leave his (Abram's) kindred to go to a land God promised him. God will always give you a symbol of the promise: a token to remember the promise. For Abram, the symbol was his name changed from Abram to Abraham. How do you believe God for something you do not have, in exchange for a promise He has given you?

Maybe you are searching for immediate deliverance from an offsetting battle?

Perhaps you beg for God's immediate presence to deliver you from a combative situation. You have been held hostage to a pernicious enemy for so long, it leaves you hanging onto your life by a strand of hair. All the devourer has to do is cut the strand and you are finished. Will God arise, or will He remain low key? Does He notice your pain? Has He seen your tears, frustration, and ailments? Does God believe that you have learned whatever He has been trying to teach you? Does your cry consist of, "GOD DON'T YOU SEE I'VE BEEN IN THIS BATTLE LONG ENOUGH? I'VE LEARNED; I'M SORRY, PLEASE HELP! DELIVER ME!" Do you sigh this aloud as each globule tear falls down the curves of your face, shedding a glimpse of internal catastrophe you must endure to win? Oh, yes, you are vulnerable!

Or could it be that you have money and a lovely home, but no peace? Maybe you have a fine home, a beautiful family, drive the finest of cars, but you long for internal fulfillment. You have all the luxuries you have ever desired; yet, you are still broken.

There is nothing more incomprehensible in life than to have everything you felt would complete you, and once you obtain them, you are still incomplete. You do not have any internal substance to anchor your weary soul. Your soul has become an abyss to so much junk it leaves you with a nauseated feeling. You have been sojourning life like a neglected child. You seek the Father only when it feeds your convenience. You only have knowledge of who He is without an intimate relationship with Him. Therefore, there is a vacancy inside you that presents you unequipped for life.

How can a person be overtly successful externally, and adversely struggling internally? How can someone be living on the exterior, and their interior constantly dieing? Oh, boy, can you put on a show for the people, but when the fun STOPS—then what? It is back to living in internal brokenness.

Where do you go from here? Matthew 23:27 put it like this, *"For ye are like unto whited sepulchers, which indeed appear beautiful outward, but are within full of dead men's bones, and of all uncleanness."* Oh, dead men's bones! Matthew said you are full of the cold, deteriorated, and dried bones that lack any luster to make them presentable. Maybe you desire the peace that comes through spiritual relationship with God. Perhaps you need to be cleansed of all that junk inside you, so that God will have a clean vacant room to occupy.

Wherever you have assessed you are, you know God must have something better. He must have something more. For some reason your circumstance displays a bitter taste to your spirit. Deep in your spirit, you know the circumstance you are in, cannot be pleasing to God. *"For we have not an high priest which cannot be touched with the feelings of our infirmities; but was in all points tempted as we are, yet without sin" (Hebrews 4:15).* Based on this Scripture we know that through the godly spirit which links us to God, if the circumstance is not pleasing to the spirit of God that dwells in us; it is not pleasing to God. Sometimes, we just have to allow God to do what He is doing in our life. Though He feels our pain and can identify with our frustrations, we have to allow Him to build us according to His pleasure. If He snatched us out of every battle we would never become the men and women God designed us to become. The potter is molding us through our battles. *"The earth is the LORD's and the fullness thereof; the world, and they that dwell therein" (Psalms 24:1).* Allow God to be God. God owns everything. He is God over our life, as well as, our "stuff."

You Need a Seed

The fact that you live in vulnerability, gives way to God to access your account. I was in a situation where life had me backed up so deep in a corner, that the only way I would escape wrath was by-way of God's mercy. The enemy tried to totally disassemble my life. He waited until I was at my lowest common denominator, then he (the enemy) pressed me beyond measure. I got bruised, bent, accumulated scratches, but I held onto my trust in God. I believed God would rescue me from the calamity. During this time period, I had suicidal thoughts. I was drowning in the storms of life. I did not see a way out . . .no help, no rescue team, and no life saving gimmicks.

Through spiritual understanding, God began to show me how cunning the enemy is. When I was about eight years old, I remember seeing my grandmother hiding a nickel-plated handgun in a closet. Twelve years later, I was at a low period devising ways to escape life. The enemy reminded me what I had witnessed twelve years before at age eight. The enemy waited until I was extremely bent out of shape before he rushed in to destroy me. The enemy was so keen to expose me to something at such young age.

He tried to use what I saw early in life, at age eight, to destroy me twelve years later. He planned on using what I saw to cease me from getting to a future he could foresee. All I had was a seed to bank on: a "mustard seed of faith" in God. *"And he said to the woman, thy faith hath saved thee; go in peace" (Luke 7:50).* That one seed helped save me from committing suicide. In your deepest vulnerability, you must hold on to your seed. My seed of faith in God helped keep me secure.

Your seed of faith is such a precious gem in your life. It holds so much power. A mustard seed is as small as a sesame seed (the seeds we see on hamburger buns). Jesus declared this size of faith was powerful enough to move one of your biggest obstacles. Wherever you have lack in your life, it is going to take faith to fill that void. You must have faith that God knows the best way to fill your void. If you try to fill it, you will fail. It might work in the beginning, but it will eventually turn out to be a dud of progress.

God wants you to be balanced. If you lack the weight of a seed on the right side of your balance beam, you need to dig deep down inside yourself and find the seed you need. The absence of this seed can leave you unbalanced.

I can remember going grocery shopping with my granddaddy. He would fill a plastic bag with beans, and set the bag on a weighing scale that was hanging in the air. He would add and subtract until he got exactly the amount of beans he wanted. I could not understand why the man could never just grab a few scoops full, and leave the area. I always noticed a big clock was sitting above the silver bowl, in which he put the bag of beans. The only time the clock hand would move was when he put the bag inside the bowl, or took the bag out of the bowl.

Later, as I got older I realized there was a price per pound on all the goods in that area. I understood my granddad was trying to balance the beam as close to one pound as he could. If he had to take away a little, he did that. Whatever it took to get the amount to where he was satisfied was the key. The same principle is what God desires for your life. You have the opportunity to put your trust in Him for everything, or you can let Him subtract those things from you that keep you from totally trusting in Him. He will subtract the things from your life that you believe in more than you believe in Him. God does not want to see you leaning more to the left because of your possessions, while your right side is suffering in spiritual growth.

I told you earlier, God would rather for you to suffer financially and be spiritually healthy. He can work with a person in that particular state. God can lead you into financial wealth through your spiritual relationship. It is hard for God to teach you balance, if you are concerned more about building your wealth, than about building your spirit. You have to look deep inside yourself, to humble yourself enough, to know you still need God to help you balance your life. You must humble yourself enough to allow God to build your spirit to equality with your health, and prosperity.

Built Through Battles

We often wish we had the potency Jesus has. We desire to perform miracles, such as, the power to glide on the face of a sea. We marvel at the power that springs from Jesus' voice when He commanded demons to flee. We covet the strength of His replies to traditionalized saints. When thoughts arise for us to walk in a similar manner to His cross obedience, we twitch!

For the saint, we have knowledge of each feat previously described. At Jesus' performances we marvel, we covet, and we twitch. For the unsaved, the only thing you may be aware of, is that Jesus was an extraordinary Man who performed miracles like walking on water. Your Sunday school teacher may have told you the Pharisees were like traditional saints that tried to keep an untraditional God under traditional rules. You might have heard Jesus was nailed to the cross and died. The effects remain the same; you marvel, you covet, and you twitch.

Every battle that confronts us in life is purposed for our growth. I do not think any of us would mind being wealthy on both sides of the beam: in spirituality, and financially. It would be nice for a person to look at us from every angle and notice the splendid job God is doing in our life. This reminds me of a diamond.

A diamond is a good example of what God

expects us to resemble. A diamond is such a beautiful gem to gaze upon. It is just as marvelous on the inside. To hold a diamond and peek through the outer encasement into its inner development makes one marvel at its beauty. A diamond is priceless. We may find grace and buy a diamond for a hundred dollars, or we can end up paying millions of dollars. We men, can be irresponsible, and unemotional—so lets use a woman.

When a woman owns a diamond, it becomes precious to her. She will store it in a safe place. She does not want to lose it, because it holds a dear place in her heart. She will not share her diamond with anyone, or lend it to anyone. It is hers. If someone close to her buys the diamond for her, it will become more significant. The diamond has a rich financial value, and it holds great internal value. It is valuable in money, and the diamond itself is valuable. What a diamond God wants you to be!

He knows we have great financial value, because we are His creation. God also wants us to know about the value we have within ourselves. A lot of us have no true idea of how valuable we are. It does not help God to know that someone dear to Him bought us for Him. Even If God wanted to leave us He couldn't, because of the price He paid for us. We were bought with a price. *"For ye are bought with a price: therefore glorify God in your body, in your spirit, which are God's" (I Corinthians 6:20).*

Do you remember when you had emotional ties to an old relationship, because of all the things you did for that boyfriend or girlfriend? You just could not let go of them. The more you tried to let go, the more it hurt to let go. It did not help you, because you practically gave up your life for them. You must have felt like you paid a huge price for that relationship, huh?

Our relationship with God is similar. Jesus gave away His life for us (me and you). *"As the Father knoweth me, even so know I the Father: and I lay down my life for the sheep" (John 10:15).* He paid a huge price for us to have a relationship with Him. It overwhelms me to know Jesus had enough faith in us to *die* for us. He had enough faith to believe His punishment on the cross would swallow all the sins we committed, and that we would take voluntary action in relation to what He did. He was punished for what *we* did, not for something He did, and He still considers us (me and you) His friends. *"Greater love hath no man than this, that a man lay down his life for his friends" (John 15:13).* "What a friend we have in Jesus!"

What is a friend? A friend is someone that is closely acquainted with you; they go through battles with you. A friend holds trust in you, they believe in you, and they love you. They will apologize when they are wrong. When they do something unpleasing to you that caused separation in the relationship, a true friend will return to try to reconcile the relationship. Webster's New Student Dictionary defines a friend as *" . . .one attached to another by affection.*

One who is not hostile, who favors something, and a Christian member that stresses inner light."

You mean to tell me after all the mistakes we have made, God stills views us as His friends? This *is* what God thinks of us? It is true! That is why it is necessary to be deeply passionate, and to believe in God. We are to be conquerors. Jesus fought through His battles in life, and overcame His flesh through faith. We are to do the same. The only way we can be conquerors over our battles is by our faith through Christ Jesus. *"Nay in all these things we are more than conquerors through him that loved us" (Roman 8:37).*

In fact, Jesus reiterated His conquering power over His flesh when He was preparing to die on the cross. He asked God to take the death of the cross away from Him, *"And he said, Abba, Father, all things are possible unto thee; take away this cup from me [the cup of wine symbolized the streaming blood that he would shed on the cross]: nevertheless not what I will, but what thou wilt" (Mark 14:36).* He did not want to go through the anguishing pain of death for sinners like you and me. In spite of our wrong He forgave us, and died to save a relationship He felt was still worthy. *"Then said Jesus, Father, forgive them; for they know not what they do" (Luke 23:34).* Jesus is God manifested in the flesh. He was actually looking deep within himself to express His forgiveness, (see I Timothy 3:16 and Hebrews 1:3).

Every battle we face is used to fashion us on the inside, so that our internal worth matches our external value. People cannot look through our outer encasement and view what is on the inside, but God can. God can see if our internal worth is flourishing or not. We are such a precious gem to God. He paid a huge price for us, so He allows us to go through battles. We have to learn how to die on our cross, lose our will, and let God's will be done for our life. *"Whosoever will come after me, let him deny himself, and take up his cross, and follow me" (Mark 8:34b).* Jesus died, but He definitely resurrected from death to live eternally (see Luke 24:20–53). The results of Jesus' death were uncontainable. Now we all have an opportunity to flourish in this life and to live eternally. If we would allow God to build us through our battles, *our* results would be uncontainable. The battles we face help us become more balanced in life.

Practical Principles

Psalms 34:17

"The righteous cry, and the LORD heareth, and delivereth them out of all their troubles."

This is a very good Scripture that reminds us that God is not incapable of hearing us. Sometimes we go through situations that cause us to believe we are in the battle alone. We all have problems that need to be solved. I tend to think that if I could just get through certain situations, my life would be so much better. I bet, at times, you tend to think in a similar fashion. I find myself in isolated zones where I quietly cry, and wonder why I have to deal with certain things.

Well the psalmist reminds us that we are not alone. In fact, he said the righteous cry and God hears our tears. Every tear that quietly falls down our face speaks loudly to God's heart. When you drop your masculinity and release genuine tears of deliverance, each tear signifies that you are truly in pain and deeply need help. God will deliver you. I cried on my way to Maryland/D.C. God heard my tears, dried my eyes, and delivered me from a troubling situation.

Psalms 34:19

"Many are the afflictions of the righteous: but the LORD delivereth him out of them all."

Have you ever been involved in something that seemed like it had no exit? Did you search, think, and try to plan you way out, without vividly seeing how you would find deliverance? Did you ever find deliverance and wonder how you were delivered? I bet you hoped you would never find yourself in a similar predicament again.

I have been in many situations like those previously described. I learned a valuable lesson from my situations; they made me a better person. Every situation I was delivered from, wiped away a little filthiness in my life, to help me live more balanced. If I got caught in a bad situation, it was probably because I made a bad decision prior to getting caught in that situation. Later in life, if a similar situation arose, I have been able to use my prior experiences to help alleviate getting into another bad situation.

Then there are some things that come upon you

that your decisions did not welcome. They are also there to help balance you.

This Scripture will help you understand that it is not foreign land, for you to go through trials. It is another reminder that trouble will come your way, but when they come, you can expect deliverance. Once you are delivered, hopefully, you will have learned something. The afflictions should challenge you to become a better person.

Summary Prayer

Lord, hear my cry. I realize that I have to go through battles. I need You to comfort me. Tuck me away in Your covering presence. You promise You will deliver me from my troubles. I believe Your promise. I do not know when deliverance from_____(your trouble) will come, but I believe deliverance is on the way. Show me what it is You want me to learn from my battles. Help me grow to live a more balanced life.

Chapter 4

Faithastrophy

Many times we believe God for huge blessings and miss the small testimony. We believe God to deliver us from the root of poverty by believing Him for an instant miracle. Some of you have missed the fact that *somehow* ten dollars stretched throughout the week, and you never missed a meal. For others, *God* stretched ten dollars for *you and your children* throughout the week.

Some of you are so caught up with your job that you have overlooked the fact that one thing can make the whole organization fall apart. God has shown us that one incident can change the course of our lives through the incident that happened with America on 9/11. Whatever the situation is that you are dealing with, your situation leaves you in deep misery, sometimes causing you to live life ahead of the literal day you are in. You are trying to elude today's trouble—which makes you constantly prep for the next day ahead. You can't enjoy today, because you are constantly trying to escape the problems that are attached with "your" today.

We find ourselves on Monday trying to figure out how to survive Tuesday and Wednesday. Monday has not even started, and here we are worried about surviving Wednesday. Matthew wrote, *"Take therefore no thought for the morrow: for the morrow shall take thought for the things of itself. Sufficient unto the day is the evil thereof" (Matthew 6:34).*

Matthew declares that *today* is a big enough battle to fight, and that our trying to *fight* tomorrow is irrelevant; it is virtually impossible. He says there is enough evil and calamity during the day at hand. We do not have time to worry about making it tomorrow. As a matter of fact, tomorrow is not promised to us. While we are spending time making preparations for tomorrow, we miss the grace God reveals to us on a daily basis.

The additive of a negative tomorrow to what we feel is currently a burden causes a mental overexertion. Therefore, Matthew says do not worry about fighting tomorrow's battle. We cannot allow the enemy to weigh down our spirits with his tactics and schemes. The enemy knows we are struggling; trying to endure today, and he will add negative thoughts about our tomorrow. The enemy will display a negative perception about our situation. We must realize that when the enemy gives us a display, it will be an over-exaggerated display. He specializes in using circumstances to deter our focus. The adversary will use our circumstance to lead us astray from our Creator

(God). He will use a mind- boggling circumstance to cause various sicknesses to develop; like stress. He also understands if he can persuade us to worry about the circumstance, our worrying will strangle our faith. Once he causes us, through his tactics, to assassinate our faith, our hope is aborted.

Faith is our spiritual foundation. Hope is the desire to obtain something. I felt like the chapter title "faithastrophy" was logical because it combines the basis with an obtained desire. It combines our *faith,* with the obtained desire—which is what we "once" hoped for. When we obtain an item that we once hoped for; that item becomes our *trophy,* or our reward. It shows **faith-as**-our only way to obtain the **trophy**; we get a trophy after we accomplish the task.

A young lady might say one day she wants to be a doctor. The day she becomes a licensed doctor it becomes something she once hoped for, but has now attained. The belief that she could become a doctor is what fueled her to accomplish her dream. Once she becomes a doctor this is her reward, or her *trophy.* Her faith has been rewarded with the trophy of what she was hoping she would achieve.

We start building whatever we *hope* for on the foundation of our faith. We start building what we *dream* of (hope) on the belief (faith) that we can accomplish what we dream.

"Hope deferred maketh the heart sick: but when the desire cometh it is a tree of life" (Proverbs 13:12). This aborted hope depletes any evidence of what you once believed you would achieve. With

all your strength you must do whatever it takes to keep hold of your faith. *"Now faith is the substance of things hoped for, the evidence of things not seen" (Hebrews 11:1).* The growth of our faith is predicated on the basis of our hope. If we hope for big things, we must have big faith. If we have no faith, the things we hope for contain no energy. Our hope, absent faith, is without nutrition. Our faith is the ignition switch to spark the motor. The things we hope for cannot live without faith.

In verse six Apostle Paul says, *"But without faith it is impossible to please him: for he that cometh to God must first believe that he is and that he is a rewarder of them that diligently seek him."* No matter what we are dealing with, our faith undergirds whether or not we reach our goal. Our lack of faith demotes our prowess to move God on our behalf. Paul shares with us that "without faith it is impossible to please God." If God is not pleased, He does not move on our behalf. Just ask the Israelites!

Under the leadership of Moses, the Israelites obtained a promise from God. God told Moses to send out chief men from the twelve tribes of Israel to spy out the land of Canaan. Canaan, for the Israelites, was the land of promise. After God delivered the Israelites from the foreign land of oppression; Egypt, He promised to move them to the glorious land of Canaan. Canaan was described as, "the land that flowed with milk and honey." Canaan was the dreamland for the Israelites. After going through hellish chaos with the Egyptians, they received a promise from God. This promise painted a beautiful portrayal of a rich soiled, water nourished, wholesome land that they only dreamed of.

After departing Egypt, they were moving forward to meet with destiny; so they thought. They later found themselves in a much worse position than being controlled by the Egyptians. Instead of resting in the glorious land of Canaan, they fell into the hands of the wilderness.

Have you ever been in a place so bad, you could not understand why you were there? Was that place so bad that you prayed, begged, and cried for deliverance? Did you feel that God would deliver you and provide for you a better place, only to find yourself in a worse place? That was the place of wilderness for Israel. They were delivered from the Egyptians to have a date with the wilderness. What a distraught feeling they must have felt! The wilderness required the Israelites to live by a substance they could not naturally comprehend. They had to walk, live, and function by *faith.*

While in the wilderness, the Israelites started losing focus. They started murmuring against Moses and God's provisions for them. It was so uncomfortable they requested to go back to the Egyptians. They wanted to know why God delivered them from the Egyptians to deliver them to die in the wilderness.

Has God ever tried to move you from destruction to destination and you questioned His motive? Whenever He (God) touches our comfort zone we get a little antsy, don't we? It does not matter if it is

God or man; we do not like to be moved from our comfort zones.

The Israelites found themselves in an uncomfortable situation, which required them to believe that God would honor His vow to them. There was no sign of a Promise Land, no sign of positive change; no sign of God, or His promise.

So God told Moses to choose choice men from every tribe of Israel. Regarding these men, Moses was instructed to send them to spy out the Canaan land. Moses did just as God asked him. He gathered rulers over each tribe, and sent them (12) to bring back reports of the land. When they returned with the report, they acknowledged that Canaan was truly a land of promise. This was exactly what God said it would be, "a land that flowed with milk and honey!" They not only saw the resources, but also saw an enemy occupying the land. This frightened the Israelites, to the extreme that their faith was totally diminished. Everyone came back with a negative report with the exception of two men: Caleb and Joshua.

Many of the rulers who were among the twelve, said the people were too strong, cities were walled, and the Anaks were living there. The Anaks were a people of great strength and mighty in stature. The Anaks were described as giants. Caleb tenaciously rebutted the argument of the fearful ones, and declared they could no doubt overtake the Anaks. Caleb and Joshua tried to persuade the Israelites that God would surely give them the land, once He brought them into the land. They (Caleb and Joshua) said the Anaks and all the others in the land of Canaan were bread for them. They (Caleb and Joshua) believed they would defeat the Anaks with God on their side. What great faith to see your giants as bread! The Israelites rejected the encouraging words of truth that Caleb and Joshua presented. In fact, the Bible says they desired to s*tone* Caleb and Joshua.

God became so furious with the Israelites lack of faith, He was going to disinherit them and move His protecting hand from over them. Moses was a man who God admonished and spoke with face to face. He asked God not to disinherit His children. God listened, but none of the current Israelites moved into the Promised Land except Caleb and Joshua.

God boasts on our faith in Him. On the contrary, if we show no faith He does not move on our behalf.

One of the worst positions in life to dwell, is a place where we feel unappreciated. If someone we are trying to assist, gives off the vibe that they do not *need* our assistance, it induces a useless feeling. Even if we *know* they need help, their making us feel useless is a slap in the face. How much more our God? He knows all about our needs, and our wants. Our faith acknowledges to God we need His help. It is a silent confession to God that the only way positive change will occur is if He moves on our behalf. That is why Paul says that without faith it is impossible to please God. Aborted faith unveils to God our lack of need for Him. We are telling God we are in control of our situations, and we have the power to alter them to our liking. You do not want to give God such impression do you?

Sustaining Faith

Our faith is extremely imperative in enduring each battle we face. While going through different battles in life we accumulate testimonies. We find prophets, such as Abraham, divulge God's grace by building *altars* as memorials. We retain memorial altars of what God gracefully brought us through. Even before we decided to donate our life to God, we ought to be able to look back and make record of His manifested grace. You might have erected an *altar* to specifically remember the time you fell asleep on the highway and He woke you in up in the nick of time, or the time we escaped gun fire and we know the bullet had our name on it. What about the divorce you did not think you would survive, or the empty pockets you continued eating on, or how about the wayward child that miraculously made a turn around. These are all memorials (altars) of God's manifested grace.

I recall one of my associates telling me a true story he was involved in when he was young. He rec-ollected the time; during a cold snowy day, he and his family were out completing business issues. He could remember sitting in the backseat with one of his brothers, while his mom was driving and, his aunt inherited the passenger seat. It was so cold that the snowy streets had converted to ice. While the snow bombarded the pavement, the car lost traction. He and the others were overcome with panic. He said immediately his mom shouted the words "JESUS!" With an elated facial expression he says, "And the car just straightened up!" This experience is one where God's immediate help was manifested, and everyone within the car beheld God's grace.

In this situation, we find a woman, this mother, who put her faith into motion. She exemplified a woman who possessed enough faith to move God. She immediately acknowledged God by His emi-nency. She placed God's ultimate authority over what she faced. As a result, she reaped a quick bene-fit; her car "straightened up." Then, she accumulated a testimony toward God's deliverance. Not only does *she* have a testimony, everyone in the car reaped the benefit of her faith. They, too, have an individual tes-timony.

Although God does not always deliver us as quick as He did in my associate's case, He still desires to take us from faith to faith. *"For therein is the righ-teousness of God revealed from faith to faith: as it is written the just shall live by faith" (Romans 1:17).* That is why He will never put more on us than we can bear. The battles we encounter are determined by the faith we possess. The amount of faith we obtain is enough to help us survive our current storm.

In this illustration, let's translate faith into gas, and your storm as going from your house to your job. You do not know if you have enough gas in the car to get to work the following morning. You get in the car and notice that the gas needle is hugging the empty status. You do not have any monetary means to add gas, but you trust that you are going to make it on what you have in the tank. Your job is at least thirty minutes away; gas needle is almost past empty sign, but you trust you will make it. One second, you fathom running out of gas sitting on the highway side, the next second, you believe you are going to fulfill the journey. While driving, you are watching the gas hand, praying, and believing. The closer you get, the more obstacles you incur—you end up in a traffic jam, or you get held up by traffic lights.

When you are in a rush, it seems like traffic lights get longer, doesn't it?

As you get closer you notice the gaslight comes on. With the appearance of the gas light and the traffic obstacles, your faith decreases. As your faith decreases, fear increases. The rising fear is what tries to sidetrack your faith. In spite of your fears, you eventually make it to your job site.

This is symbolic to facing life's battles. We have at least enough faith to make it through our current trial. When our faith light comes on, God's strength coincides and carries us through. Once we make it through the battle, our faith builds and we become deeper enriched for the next battle. Each conquered battle increases our faith. As we conquer battles we move from faith to faith. As our faith increases, our strength increases.

On account of previous battles we have survived, our strength from those battles becomes useful to defeat our current battle. If we run out of strength,

God's strength intervenes. *" For my strength is made perfect in weakness" (II Corinthians 12:9).* The battles we face, in many cases, are designed to strengthen us. They are designed to mold and build us.

Exercise Your Weakness

"The glory of young men is their strength . . .the beauty of old men is their grey head" (Proverb 20:29). Society illuminates that carved muscles are associated with having a good looking body. The proverb declares this is a young man's glory; the way his body looks, his physicality, and his increase in strength.

Before any person steps into the weight room, his mind is set on what is about to take place. He is about to lift weights for a better look and feeling. A weight-lifter knows, in order to develop physically, he must lift weights. To increase his muscle mass he must apply pressure to the area he desires to build. If he wants to increase the chest volume, he must use weight and repetitiously focus on angles centering on building the chest. Through this repetitive process and increasing the weight, the chest increases in mass and volume.

The weight-lifter's confidence increases as his strength increases. Through the repetitive process of weight lifting, the lifter increases their strength. He may start out with twenty pounds of weight—a few weeks later he increases to thirty pounds. About a month later he has leaped to lifting over one hundred pounds of weight. As he increases weight, the weight places unfamiliar restraint against the body. This weight restrain is what builds the mass of the muscle. The more he lifts, his muscles gain familiarity with the process.

As he increases his strength, he will start noticing changes in different areas of the body. The pressure to push the weight from the body causes the muscles to work and contract. It is the lifter battling the weight. Of course, the weight has no mind to defeat him nor destroy him, but the weight still has the ability to injure or hurt the lifter. The weight is designed to mold and build the weight-lifter. The weight-lifter knows he is about to use painful circumstances for his *benefit.*

Many times when a beginner is introduced to the gym he may endure this painful battle for a little while. After he has tried to hang in the game for a little while, he may decide to abort the process.

Once he deviates from the weight-lifting battleground, the strength he worked so hard to gain, begins to decrease. If he lifted three hundred pounds, a few days away from the gym impedes the progress; so much so that he will find himself no longer lifting three hundred pounds but reduced to two hundred and fifty-five pounds. This decline occurs because of inconsistency. Once he aborts the weight-lifting process he begins to lose gained ground.

Weight-lifting is an engagement that takes time, effort, and discipline. It takes all three elements to acquire the look one desires, gain the good looking attributes, and reap the accomplishments. It is a long, and sometimes tedious process.

When we abort the process we stagnate the promise. What is the promise? The promise for the weight-lifter is refined muscles, provided he follows the proper guidelines. He understands that in order to reap the benefit, he must withstand the process. He has to go through immense pain, share his time, and remain disciplined. All three elements can cause the weight-lifter to abort the process.

Beginners who are new to weight-lifting find out that weight-lifting hurts while training, and it also hurts while relaxing. They learn that while doing the reps they must endure pain. The next day they are extremely sore on account of yesterday's painful process. The process just plain hurts, and people abort the process because of the strenuous pain.

Time is essential in the process. The weight-lifter must manage a system to fit his schedule, or his time will become an issue. He will begin trying to fit in unavailable time causing a dysfunctional schedule. The amount of time the weight-lifter spends in the gym determines the time it takes to reach the goal. He cannot spend less time, nor can he over exert himself. If he spends less time he will never reach his goal; if he spends too much time lifting, his muscles will become exhausted, and will not grow due to lack of rest. The process bids the muscles to grow. They cannot grow because the food they are being feed (referring to the reps and weight) is too much at one time. You cannot feed an eight month-old baby three spoons of applesauce at one time.

It also requires coherent discipline to stay on track. A lack of discipline will ignite the decision to abort the entire process. If the weight-lifter fails to understand the risk of being undisciplined, he will abort the promise. Being undisciplined will cause him to lose focus on the goal and step off track. If he begins missing scheduled days, he will not see the results he is looking for. When the weight-lifter does not feel like going to the gym, he still must go. If he allows his feelings to sidetrack him, those feelings will cause him to waver while in the process. This wavering spirit is what begins the aborting process.

The weight-lifter may decide he does not feel like going to the gym on Monday; he will go Tuesday. He later recalls he has other plans Tuesday, so he will make up Monday and Tuesday on Wednesday. Wednesday it may be another excuse. He must alleviate lame excuses and train his mind to override his emotions. Staying on track assists the process it takes to retain what the muscles need to grow. If he misses scheduled days on a continual process, the muscles are not consistently receiving the information they require to grow. For instance:

If a student has an exiting exam in a month and she only studies for a small amount of time, she will lose knowledge of the information that is required to pass the exam. The student has to exercise her mind on a *continual* basis in order to retain the knowledge necessary to pass the exam.

This reasoning is why our elementary teachers required us to constantly repeat and study multiplication tables. We all know how tedious studying multiplication tables can be. This constant process helped us retain the knowledge necessary to grow, obtain the data, and move to the next phase of growth. We also gave our mind rest to log in and save the information. If we lacked discipline with multiplication tables, we would have never repeated the process in order to grow. Hence, it would have made transitioning in school difficult.

Discipline fueled us to continue repeating them over and over, even when we got discouraged because we could not see results of our labor. We may have gotten angry, tossed the flash cards, or kicked the dresser; but the discipline to reach our goal kept us focused.

We look at the weight-lifter again in similar fashion; similar also to a normal person in life. If the weight-lifter lacks discipline, he will abort the process too quick when he does not see quick results. The pain he endures, his time and discipline, are all tied to his faith. The faith it takes to believe if he endures the pain, devotes his time, and stays disciplined, he will reach his goal.

The wavering spirit previously discussed, James calls "wavering faith." *"But let him ask in faith, nothing wavering. For he that wavereth is like a wave of the sea driven with the wind and tosses"* *(James 1:6)*. Wavering faith is an unstable faith. One day we might believe we can accomplish a task; the next minute we do not believe the accomplishment is possible. When we keep going back and forth in our beliefs, it is called a wavering faith. James says if we have this type of faith, the vicissitudes of life will toss us all over the place. We will come and go with no concrete stability. Then, in verse 7, James says if we have wavering faith we should not have an expectation from God. Why? I refer you back to Hebrews 11:6 which talks about our "lack of faith" not pleasing God. So hold on to your faith and do not abort the process.

Disconnect the Connection

We interact with society and the world through use of our senses. Through our sensual engagements, messages are conveyed. The way an item feels, something smells, what we hear, what something or someone looks like, or something tastes like plugs the human being into worldly sockets. Our senses give us the ability to enjoy life, while at the same time the same senses can translate messages that cause disgust with life.

Child medications for certain symptoms have a candy-like flavor. As we grow older, we find medications for the same complications, become very distasteful. The point made is, one sense can gather good message, and the same sense can receive a bad message. So we find we are moved through our senses.

We connect with God through our faith, because our faith is how we move God. Faith locks us into

God, to believe that whatever we hope for we shall obtain it. While we are able to move God through our faith in Him, the enemy moves us through our senses. The enemy yearns to detach us from our attachment to God. Therefore he (the enemy) specializes through our senses. Each sense we have, registers a message to our brain. If we grab a thorn we think . . .*hurt* . . .*sharp;* if we taste boiling water, we think, *hot;* if we see a white rose, we think, *pretty,* and the list goes on.

While I was in college I heard my college Pastor; Mr. Davis say if "he detached our head from our body, we would be useless." This is true. It would be no use for the enemy to bother us. Why? Because we would be no threat to him. He understands the closer we get to God, the farther away we move from him. The farther away we move from the enemy, the more dangerous we become to the enemy's kingdom. Everything we do in Christianity relies on our faith. To acknowledge there is a God takes faith, to get a prayer through takes faith, to believe God will answer our prayers requires faith, and to believe we will overcome our current battles, requires faith.

As previously stated, each battle we survive, builds our faith. In this Christian warfare our strength is not physical. The enemy will totally destroy us if we try to win through our own physical efforts. Our physical strength is useless. Our real strength comes from our faith. It is the only strength we can truly rely on. As a matter of fact, our faith is so strong, the smallest amount of faith can remove mountains. *"If ye have faith as a grain of mustard seed, ye shall say to this mountain, remove hence to yonder place; it shall; and nothing shall be impossible to you" (Matthew 17:20).* We can get on our knees and pray, but without faith our prayers are empty: holding no substantial weight. God wants to know we really have the sense to believe He will act on what we request.

The Battle Ground

There is a war going on for our mind. The enemy tries to defeat us through mind illusions, while God wants us to use our trust in Him to defeat the enemy. That is why Paul told the church of Corinth *"Our weapons to win this warfare are mighty through God to casting down imagination and every high thing that exalteth itself to the obedience of Christ" (II Corinthians 10:4, paraphrased).* We have to believe in God when we are down and out, facing death, or divorce. We have to exercise our weaknesses.

Sometimes the most onerous battles have a way of chipping away at our faith. Some battles seem like they may never cease. That is why our testimonies hold such power. Our testimonies provide us an obligated reason to continue in the struggle. We know what Jehovah is capable of doing. Therefore, even the residue of our faith has the ability to keep God's attention. Just like the weight-lifter and the math student we must exercise our weaknesses to build them up, while staying on track through our faith in God.

The more battles we overcome, the more our faith in God develops. Our faith in God should promote us into a deeper relationship with God. Every battle that becomes our grave burial, should strengthen our case for God's sovereignty. Every time the enemy tries to bribe us, we should be able to point him toward one of our resurrected grave sights. During the first stages of our Christian walk, it may have been easy for the devil to bait us. He probably used fear of some situation, or reminded us how good pre-marital sex was to cause us to backslide. The more we understand God's love for us, and come to realization that His grace suffices; the closer we will gravitate toward God.

The enemy desires to keep our blinders closed, making it hard to see the smallest amount of light. As we study the Word more and more, we begin to twist the lever that opens those closed blinders. The more time we spend worshipping, praising, and praying to God the more we twist that lever. The more time we spend doing these things, the farther we separate from the enemy and his darkness. The farther we separate from darkness, the closer we get to the light. The closer we get to the light, the more connected we become to God. *"Then spake Jesus again unto them, saying, I am the light of the world: he that followeth me shall not walk in darkness, but shall have the light of life" (John 8:12).* As we become more connected to God, we become less connected to the enemy.

Our connection to God will welcome more light into our lives, and we will see less darkness. It is not that the enemy has eternally left us; it is that our interaction with light exposes his darkness. We become aware of his (the enemy's) tactics. We are disconnecting ourselves from the enemy through our connection to God.

Practical Principles

Hebrews 11:1

"Now faith is the substance of things hoped for, the evidence of things not seen."

Understand that whatever we do will take faith. Our deliverance accomplish-ments, and achieve-ments will take faith. Sometimes just having faith in people is not enough.

It is erroneous for me to be on a deathbed believing in some doctor to help me live. Though the doctor may say encouraging words, deep inside he may be thinking there is no way I will make it. Or, perhaps he believes God for a miracle that is required for me to make it. I may as well alter my faith to the Superiority. I have the opportunity to by-pass all by-standers and plug my faith into God on behalf of myself for anything I desire. Why not believe in He who is in control of the doctor, as opposed to believing in the doctor? God has given you the same benefit.

Philippians 4:19

"But my God shall supply all your need according to his riches in glory by Christ Jesus."

We do not have to want for anything. I am not only talking about finances. I am also talking about our health needs, peace of mind, or even a change in a child's attitude. God placed a lady friend in my life. She played a key role when I needed her the most. He was supplying a need of mine. God will supply all of your needs, too!

We do not often see the help He provides for us, but many times God places treasure in our life that will not appear until the time comes for it to reveal itself to us.

Summary Prayer

Dear God, strengthen my faith. I need a deeper revelation of who You are. I do not search solely for the "stuff" You can give me. I search for You—because I know I belong to You. I know that if I can find out exactly who You are, it will be easier for me to trust in You with all my might and strength. I am overwhelmed that You desire to be my total supplier. I love You so much. Strengthen me, God. I know it is a process, but help me detach totally from the enemy and to become totally attached to You.

Chapter 5

Who is Exempt?

I will attempt to sum up everything we deal with in life, by simply saying "Life!" Once again let's bring "life" to life, so that we can see more of the unrelenting mind life has toward us. If there was no God, what moves life? How do the subjects of life move us? Why is it that when we cover one blown pothole, the rising water pressure closed off from that pothole sneaks somewhere behind us to dash out of a new created pothole. Once we get that one closed off, another one forms.

Life is mindless of everyone who is introduced to it. We become entangled with our individual problems. We, oftentimes, lose conscience that our neighbors also battle life. We often wonder whether or not others are dealing with troubles similar to our own.

Could the couple down the street be dealing with more than what you are dealing with? The lady down the street is wealthy, looks good, and consistently smiles. Is she exempt from life's challenges?

You are sure others have their problems, but

question whether their battles are as challenging as yours.

Who is exempt? Exactly who is exempt from the crushing wind blows that uppercut us while we are looking for a straight right-handed jab? Isn't it just like life to sneak up on us, and present us with something we did not expect? Of course, I am not talking about an unexpected birthday present. I am referring to the ticking time bombs that await our attention; devices meant to devour our lives.

The people who are often known to be battling destruction, are those who live in poverty. We can look at them, their lifestyle, the shelter they reside in, and almost assume they are less fortunate. We can gaze upon them and tell they have a daily battle with life—trying to survive. Sometimes, when a person hears the word "Africa," pre-conceived thoughts immediately arise. Even though everyone in Africa is not struggling with poverty, the pictures we constantly view via television or magazine media, convey such images. Sometimes, even, they (people in poverty) are over-looked. We have become comfortable seeing people in financial poverty. We are numb to them. It is disdainful to think, *"As long as it is not us living in poverty things are okay."* Let's not get above ourselves. God provided enough grace for us not to live in such mode.

What about the middle-class to upper-upper class people—are they exempt? Even people such as high profile athletes, movie stars, corporate company owners, or blue-collar workers that live very comfortably have battles to face. It is folly to believe that our money, will exempt us from problems. We often overlook those in poverty, and look past those that are wealthy when it comes to battling life. We accept the notion that poverty-stricken people will always be in their situation, and we believe the wealthy are exempt from life's battles. I can assure you that life does not think as we think. Life is totally mindless of us!

There was a time when King David sent the children of Israel out to war. He sent Joab (who was his acting general), his servants, and all Israel to fight the Ammonites. While Israel was out waging war, David tarried in Jerusalem. David arose from his bed to go to the top of the house. He looked over from the top of the roof and saw a woman. The Bible says she was a beautiful woman. As David beheld her beauty, he sent messengers to notify the woman that he wanted to see her. By far, would a woman reject mail sent from the "King"! This woman happened to be Bathsheba, the wife of Uriah, one of David's foreign army commanders.

David had sex with Bathsheba, a married woman. After the incident, she left, only to discover that sin was waiting to expose her—Bathsheba was pregnant. She sent a message to tell David what happened, because of their encounter. David sent a message to Joab to release Uriah from the war to come back to Jerusalem. David and Uriah began to converse with one another. They finished their discussion, and David released Uriah to depart for home.

David, expected Uriah to go home to lay with his wife, (the child would easily be perceived as Uriah's, if the couple were intimate soon). However, David discovered that instead of returning to his own house following their meeting, Uriah slept at the king's house with the other servants. Uriah was humble enough not to engage in home entertainment with his wife, while his counterparts were still out at war. David understood Uriah's reasoning for not going home. David then tried to get Uriah drunk, thinking he would foolishly go home to sleep with his wife. Once again, Uriah slept with the other servants the following night.

What will the King do next?

David sent a letter to Joab by Uriah. In the letter, David ordered Joab to put Uriah on the frontline of the most violent battle. He told Joab to isolate Uriah while in battle, so that he would be killed during the battle. Joab followed the King's orders. Uriah was killed during battle.

Under the Hebrew law, a woman could be free to re-marry only if her husband died. David must have known this. He orchestrated Uriah's death to free Bathsheba from her marriage. This way it would appear that David got Bathsheba pregnant under perfect rights of being legally married. Once again David tried to cover up his sin.

This displeased God. God sent His prophet Nathan with a message, specifically, for David. Nathan told David the following parable of two men. One of the men was rich, and the other was poor. The rich man had many things in his possession, while the poor man had only one thing in his possession. This was the only thing that had ever been with the poor man: it was a *ewe* lamb. The poor man nourished her, raised her, and spent quality time with her. They had become so intimate with one another, she was not only his friend; she was like one of his own.

Nathan said one day a traveler came along. This traveler went to the rich man. Instead of the rich man giving the traveler a sacrifice from his possessions, the rich man took what the poor man had and gave it to the traveler. He gave the traveler the poor man's biggest investment: his only lamb.

David became enraged with anger at what this rich man had done, only to find out that his anger was directed to himself. Nathan was sent by God to convict David of his wrongdoing. He told David, "You are this man that has done such!" This parable was written in this book, not to expose David, or to kindle sorrow for Uriah. It was re-recorded to show you, *no one* is exempt from life.

David would have never seen himself, if life had not shown up. In the midst of wondering about the outcome of the war, arose unseen problems. David went from one broken situation to another. Though his problems could have been alleviated, the fact that life is mindless of people remains.

You may have been able to *buy* your way out of certain battles. You may have enough political power to *cover up* a lot of your dirty tracks. There are battles you will discover that payments cannot alleviate, nor can your power overcome. David was, obviously, rich. If he were not rich, it would have been irrelevant for God to send David a word to compare him to a rich man. God used a parable that connected David to something to which he could relate. He used a parable that would help David see himself, and convict him of what he had done. David probably overlooked what the outcome would be in the beginning. Later he uncovered the seriousness of remaining obedient to God.

On the opposite end of this story, we are introduced to a woman that was initially isolated from her husband by a war. They must have been extremely close, due to the parable Nathan told David. The parable was the story of a poor man fully concentrated on the only companion in his life. She went from isolation to feeling like she betrayed her husband. She was probably thoroughly disgusted with knowing she committed adultery. She probably felt dirty, confused, and used. Bathsheba was taken advantage of because of her beauty. She knew her husband had invested quality and effort into their relationship. She may have felt the least she could do to show her appreciation was to remain undefiled and pure for her husband. Bathsheba found herself going from loneliness, to misery, to being depressed.

David tried to cover the pothole, only to birth another pothole. Because of David's sin, he dealt with such battles. It does not, necessarily, have to be sin that causes problems to arise in our life. It can be the fact that God is moving us into a new stage of growth. We must fight our battles in life in order to survive. We have to learn how to be built up (up) through the battles we face.

Our seniority does not exempt us; our beautiful looks do not permit us benefits when fighting a battle. The depth of our wealth does not drown our situations. I am not exempt; you are not exempt; neither is that person we might compare our problems to. As a matter of fact, we counsel our problems to increase when we compare ourselves to others. The problems we have are designed for *our* individual growth. We need not to season our problems by shaking a dash of our neighbor's current status onto our own.

A Deceptive Power

The grasp of money leads us to believe that once we have it, problems disappear. Sure money will alleviate a lot of bills. Of course, money will provide opportunities to enjoy life. What affects our increase with financial wealth is the wisdom to remain self-controlled when using it, or the trust we have in it. Poor people want to know how to get rich, and rich people want to know how to overcome what they are dealing with. Basically, both parties want a resolution to the problems they face.

Some poor people are blinded to believe financial wealth is a total resolution. *Some* rich people are misled to believe money is always the key. If this does not describe you, I release you to move to the next chapter. Otherwise, allow these words held within to help nourish you. (I do not make these assessments to put all poor or rich people into one box. This is just a general assessment to make the point that we all have problems).

We dwell on a world where everyone is pulled by the chain of the dollar. How much can you get for your assistance? This is the question that develops in our society. We witness multiple lawsuits, and see cases unravel because of the financial value of a person. Even if we know a person is living a lie, we look past righteous for wickedness!

Certain people commit indecent acts, because they know their power is the key to their liberation. They know it because the world constantly looses them from the disasters they face. Some rich people try to hide behind their wealth. I have no numerical statistics to back my point, nor do I need them. I know this to be true because of "the statistic" held within my Bible. The Bible says, *"The rich man's wealth is his strong city" (Proverbs 10:15)*. The word declared it before we realized it in life. This exploit that the scripture declared has passed from generation to generation. We continue to see the rich hide behind their wealth today. *All* rich people do not have this gross thinking; nor does every person in poverty believe money is the only resolution. Nevertheless, the problem is still alive.

I have written to tell you financial wealth is useless when you are fighting against life. What do you do when you have everything life offers, and you still lack internal fulfillment? Where do you go when you own much, but you lose your family? How does someone walk with their head held high, while their heart is completely shattered? *"Charge them that are rich in this world, that they be not high-minded, nor trust in uncertain riches, but in the living God, who giveth us richly all things to enjoy" (I Timothy 6:17).*

Life will back us into a corner that will bring us to realization that financial wealth really never is/was a safe haven. After we have fought, sweat, and pushed to become a financial success; life will deflate the hot air in our balloon. For some, a deflating balloon is too slow to describe what happened to them. Life snatched the chair right from under them. We must not ever become so high-minded that we believe we are exempt from battles. We are not exempt.

When I began this chapter, God led me to deal with financial wealth. He wants to expose the uncovered facts of wealth without Him. I started to write a message about the rich hiding behind their wealth. At a certain point I ran into a brick wall. I had ideas of what to write next, but none of the ideas seemed to fit the shoe. I had no exact flow to get the precise point across in this regard to meet the need. I wondered what do I write next? I will tell you.

I work with mental health patients. Everyday I deal with patients that struggle to find the solutions to their problems. I authorize them to see psychiatrist, psychologist, counselors, or attend a variety of different mental health institutions. There is no significant time to discuss their problems with them, nor is that my task to do so. I did not know what to say next in this book, or how to say it. I meditated, prayed, and asked God questions about what to write. In the midst of seeking what God wanted me to say next, my answer appeared. He answered my question through one of my patients!

It happened to be around 4:30 P.M., when I got a call from a man. He asked me to give him a general overview of what he could be looking at (cost) regarding counseling. He wanted to know what his insurance policy would cover should he decide to see an out-of-network counselor (a counselor not contracted with the patient's insurance). He and I begin to talk. He immediately wrapped his hand around my attention when he told me his situation.

Richard describes himself as a street kid from Brooklyn that came up the hard way. He believes he is a survivor that fought for everything he ever accomplished. Over the course of time, he managed to become a financial success in life. He had gotten married, had a daughter, had an eighty-thousand-dollar per year job (excluding wife's income), owned two homes, had many cars, was able to buy his wife whatever she wanted. He also had a child that never lacked anything. He was happy and successful.

Richard could stare life in the face and wag his head at his early Brooklyn struggles. Everything he missed during his early stages in life, he eventually overcame. Man, did life lose conscience of this financially successful businessman! He was a wealthy, loving, family oriented success. That is until life robbed him of his success. Richard's years of labor pains to become a success, came to a screeching halt in a matter of days. It must have seemed like he went to sleep in a bed of roses, only to awake in the thorns of a bush.

What happened? What went wrong? How could life be so dramatic?

His loving wife for thirty-two years became handicapped and was put in a wheel chair; she, eventually died. He lost his daughter to her deathbed; he lost his high paying job, his cars, his houses, and everything else he owned. This man, even began to lose his mind. He started giving everything, and anything away. This loving man transitioned into an angry, careless, weeping madman.

As I partook of his pain, I shared with him my deep appreciation for him. Richard is definitely a survivor. I told him I needed him to survive this catastrophic battle. His one call to me will help others see the carelessness of life. Life snatched the chair from under Richard like it does so many of us. Richard is trying to fight his way to remain mentally stable. He is currently a truck driver who says he continues to give money away. Financial wealth does not have the same meaning to him, as it did years ago.

This beloved man gave me such a profound statement. He told me he often tells people, " *. . .never let a day go by without telling your loved ones that you love them. Tomorrow is not promised to us, and you never know when those you love will be taken away from you. I have nobody that loves me* *anymore. I would rather be poor with somebody who loves me, than to be rich with no fulfillment. Dee I'm glad you are writing your book. Stories like this will help a lot of people."* Those are the exact words that Richard shared with me. Life is mindless of us. A lot of the things we deal with in life just happen to us. We cannot allow financial wealth to deceive us any longer. We should not trust in something that cannot save our soul. God loves us so much, that He said if we trust in Him for who He is, He is able to give us riches to enjoy. Do not trust in financial wealth. Trust in God who supplies the financial wealth.

A Change in Trust

During Jesus' ministry, He and his disciples journeyed from Galilee to Judea. While Jesus was giving the disciples a school lesson, a certain rich ruler approached Jesus. He presented Jesus with an intriguing question. He asked, *"What good thing shall I do that I may have eternal life" (Matthew 19:15)?* Jesus began to name off a portion of the Ten Commandments for an answer. The man told Jesus that he had done each of them since he was a child. He confidently asked Jesus if he lacked anything else—being that he kept the commandments? Jesus keenly answered the ruler's question. He told the young ruler to "go sell everything he had, and give to the poor." Jesus told the man (my paraphrase) he would have treasure in heaven, so, give it all away, then come and follow Me. The ruler was broken by what Jesus told him. The Bible says the man left with great sorrow for he owned much (see Matthew 19:5).

Jesus tested the man's faith. The man must have believed he could work his way toward eternal life. He initially asked Jesus what could he "do" to live eternally. Each commandment Jesus gave him was a commandment that required action. Jesus told him *not* to commit murder, *not* to commit adultery, *not* to lie, *not* to steal, to *honor* his parents, and to *love* his neighbor as himself.

The ruler told Jesus he had done all those things, everything Jesus instructed. He was confident in himself to acknowledge to himself that his actions were in sync. He did everything the Mosaic laws commanded. He ran to Jesus, as a result of his good works. Jesus understood that the man's understanding was unaligned. Therefore, he challenged the man's understanding.

First, Jesus knew He (Jesus-Himself) was/is the only door for anyone to inherit eternal life. *Second,* Jesus understood He had to challenge the man to lose his current life to gain eternal life. *"For whosoever will save his life shall lose it: and whosoever will lose his life for my sake shall find it. For what is a man profited, if he shall gain the whole world, and lose his own soul? Or what shall a man give in exchange for his soul" (Matthew 16:25,26).* In Mathew 16:24, Jesus told His disciples that any man coming after Him must deny himself and take up his cross.

Third, Jesus also knew the man had to be a witness of who He (Jesus) was and would become. The man had to partake in Jesus' sufferings, his death, his burial, and resurrection. *"That if thou shalt confess with thy mouth the Lord Jesus, and shalt believe in thine heart that God hath raised him from the dead, thou shalt be saved (Romans 10:9)."* In other words, the ruler had to know enough about Jesus to confess Jesus as Lord. He also had to have knowledge of the crucifixion, and believe that God resurrected a dead Jesus. Glory to God! Mark 10:21 says Jesus told the ruler to take up the cross and follow Him. Involving himself in this action, the ruler would have to die to himself and lose his life. In return, he would gain knowledge of a cross bearing Jesus. He would also partake in Jesus' suffering, death, His burial, and His resurrection. That is why Jesus told the ruler to follow Him.

Matthew did not establish whether the ruler inherited his position, was appointed his position, or was granted his position as ruler. We do not know if he labored drastically for his possessions. What Matthew established is that he was a "certain rich ruler." Can you imagine yourself owning everything; sitting on top of the world? Then Jesus tells you to go sell whatever you own and give it to the poor. To hear what Jesus told you to do would be hard to conceive. Then, to actually initiate the act, takes what Jesus told you to another level.

Jesus said, *"If thou wilt be perfect, go and sell that thou hast, and give to the poor" (Matthew 19:21).* First, Jesus told him to go sell his possessions. Then He adds a conjunction with the word, "and!" Jesus did not tell the man to go sell his possessions to the poor; that would have been lame to do so. If they are already poor, obviously, they could not buy his stuff from him. Therefore, Jesus put the ruler in a *sales position* to sell to everyone except the poor. Next, the ruler was told to take the income *from* his sold possessions and *give* it to the poor.

Now we see Jesus place the ruler in a *servant-hood position. "But so shall it not be among you: but whosoever will be great among you, shall be your minister: And whosoever of you will be the chiefest, shall be servant of all (Mark 10: 43, 44)."* After he sold the possessions, received the amount, then he was told to take the amount and give it to the poor. Jesus told him to serve those that are financially below him. This action would put the ruler into a humble position. God cannot do anything with us if we are not humble enough to serve, and learn.

Last, Jesus was showing the ruler that the only way he would gain eternal life was by altering his faith. When the ruler left full of sorrow, it showed that the man had too much trust in his financial wealth. He originally approached Jesus, because he knew Jesus knew the answer to obtaining eternal life. Though *he* knew *Jesus* knew the answer, the man did not know Jesus *was* the *answer.* If he understood exactly who Jesus was, it would not have been as painful for the ruler to receive Jesus' instructions.

Jesus' disciples left their current life without any questions when they were asked to follow Jesus. Jesus told them, in the middle of what they were doing, to come and follow Him. While fishing, Peter and Andrew received the command Jesus gave them. They left their fishing nets, and followed Jesus with no questions (See Matthew 4).

The ruler really had no clue of what he was asking. According to his reaction, he must have felt like he was losing all that he had. Jesus told his disciples, *"Verily I say unto you, There is no man that hath left house, or brethren, or sisters, or father, or mother, or wife, or children, or lands, for my sake, and the gospel's, . . .But he shall receive an hundredfold now in this time, houses, and brethren, and sisters, and mothers, and children, and lands, with persecutions; and in the world to come eternal life" (Mark 10: 29,30)."*

The ruler did not realize to lose his life for a life with Jesus was actually a huge gain. To inherit what he asked from Jesus required huge faith—to let go of what he *knew* for something he *wanted.* I wonder if he wanted it bad enough. God does not want to take away what we currently have for our *loss.* He takes things away for our *gain.* He hates for us to trust in something He created for us. To walk with Jesus requires us to alter our faith. God will cultivate the garden of our life until He gets our attention. He will snatch weeds from our life, and take away anything else that does not assist with our destiny. He will allow us to end up in an isolated position until we acknowledge His presence, and learn what He wants us to learn. If your faith is not in Jesus, alter it! If He has to do it, the feeling will be more painful.

Wealthy without Completion

I question myself—what is the reason that would make someone believe God is the only answer for their problems? What is it about this book that differs from all the other books we have read? I am talking about the books that we may have read in search for solutions to our problems. There are a variety of different books available that are geared for God's people. Make no doubt about it; there are some very good books out there. Sometimes, it just does not seem like the actions certain books tell us to perform are the right solutions. Certain books motivate us, and inspire us, but the problems we have are still living with us. This book presses us into gaining a deeper relationship with God. It is a very practical book with no gimmicks, just a book promoting a substance called faith. Of course, your problems may linger. Yet, your faith is vital in sustaining you through your battle.

What good is it for a billionaire to be a billionaire if every dollar he owns is cursed? Every time he buys something, another item comes up broken. He has enough money to replace what he lost, but he walks with cursed money in his account. What good is it to be a billionaire with cursed money, and living a cursed life?

Maybe you have no reason to ask for more money due to your extreme wealth. Let me ask you this one question. Can you buy your way into heaven? I just do not believe you can roll your money over into heaven. If you died tonight, would your children say they know you went to heaven? Or would they say you are probably in hell, because you never had a relationship with God? Have your children ever seen you pray? Are your children satisfied with who you are and the life you lead? Are your children seeing a different parent in the home every so often? You may have bought your loves ones everything the world has to offer, but are *they* totally complete? Maybe they are young and immature, but do they know the proper way to *become* complete?

I want to know how to overcome my battles, and come out okay. I want to know how to come out of the battle with everything I went in with, and possibly more. I assume you want to know the same. The more I search for answers there is only one answer that develops. We overcome our battles by faith in God, through patience. *"My brethren, count it all joy whey you fall into divers temptations; knowing this, that the trying of you faith worketh patience" (James 1:2, 3).*

We have to be patient. The only way we can have perfect patience is through God. God has all the answers for our needs. God is our only strength. We cannot buy our way out of a battle; people cannot pull us out, nor can our educational degrees help us get out.

If God really wanted, He could shut the business down. He could allow death to wipe out our whole family, if He really wanted. Bankruptcy is resting at our door. Death is right around the corner. There is a kidnapper lurking to snatch away some innocent child. God forbid the child to be one of our children. I am not writing to wish evil on you. I want you to know if God is not the centerpiece of our life, then the enemy has permission to steal from us whatever he desires. Without a relationship with God, the enemy can do to us what he wants. I would hate for you to read this book, and take everything that you read lightly.

If you are internally incomplete, regardless of your wealth, chances are everything you have bought your loved ones has not completed them. The God you serve should be a direct reflection of the God they should serve. The exact God that yearns to fulfill you can fulfill your loved ones. Wouldn't it be nice to have everything you want externally, then to have complete internal fulfillment? My prayer is that you walk out your life and know the closest people in your life are equally affected by your complete lifestyle. Wouldn't it be nice to be wealthy, and not wonder if we have done everything right? I mean to be rich and joyful, as opposed to, rich and sorrowful. *"The blessing of the LORD, it maketh rich, and he addeth no sorrow with it" (Proverbs 10:22).*

God's blessing will make us rich; not only this, but He says we will not be sorry as a result. The opposite of sorrow is joy. There is no in-between with God. It is either hot or cold, good or bad, righteous or unrighteous. If you are already rich, why not deepen your trust in God for some internal joy. You already have one phase complete with your financial wealth, but maybe your inner man is impoverished. *"A good man leaveth an inheritance to his children's children" (Proverbs 13:22a).* There is nothing wrong with being rich. It would be wise to leave behind a financially rich legacy, with a spiritually rich foundation.

The reason you may be unfulfilled is because God is calling you to deepen your faith in Him. God wants us to be rich in health, in finances, in our walk, in our thinking, and in our inner-being. He wants us blessed, our spouse blessed, our children blessed, our home, cars, and pets blessed. After all, He said He would bless our seed. *"And he will love thee, and bless thee, and multiply thee: he will also bless the fruit of thy womb (our children), and the fruit of thy land, thy corn, and thy wine, and thine oil, the increase of thy kine, and the flocks of thy sheep, (all our stuff including animals, food, and pets) in the land which he sware unto thy fathers to give thee"* (Deuteronomy 7:13). God wants to intrude into your home in every aspect. We may be the reason His progress is being impeded.

You may have no need for money; maybe you just want your spouse saved. Do you believe God is capable of performing a mind-changing miracle? Deepen your trust in God. Whatever the battle is that you face, keep the faith and *"let patience have her perfect work that you may be fulfilled/complete"* (James 4:3).

There was a woman who was incomplete for twelve years straight. She had money, and she had friends, but she also had an internal issue that no one or nothing could seem to fill. I found out that this woman never stopped believing in God, she never stopped trusting in Him, and she patiently waited for

God to answer her prayer! As a result, she was finally made complete (see Mark 5:25–34).

Practical Principles

II Corinthians 2:14

"Now thanks be unto God, which always causeth us to triumph in Christ, and maketh manifest the savour of his knowledge by us in every place."

Glory, Glory in God's triumphant Glory! The apostle Paul said we must thank God who makes us victorious through every battle in Christ. This Scripture is so deep that God inspired Paul to tell us that we *smell* like victory before the battle, in the battle, and after the battle. I need not say more. This Scripture is enough to motivate you through the remainder of your test.

Colossians 2:10

"And ye are complete in him, which is the head of all principality and power."

We live a great fraction of our life without total completion. We devote our time and effort into people and/or things that are not the proper piece to filling our voids. The truth of the matter is we cannot learn how to be fulfilling to others until we learn what true fulfillment entails. We have to learn where our real fulfillment resides, before we can extract what we need. When we learn where the supply is, we can share the supply with others.

Summary Prayer

Father - Thank you graciously for the words of wisdom you have bestowed. God, I accept who You are, and who You desire to be in my life. I want to bask in Your triumphantly glory. Search me, God, as I search You. I search for You for the true fulfilling presence You want to become in my life. Hold my hand as I walk through the battle. Guide me through the darkness of the day. Shield me with Your powerful manifestation. I trust You, God.

Chapter 6

The Gardener

A lonely little girl meanders down a rural road. She is new in the small country town. This new town presents her void of friendship, laughter, and love. She decides to walk to the local park that her parents previously escorted her to just days before; fun definitely waits for her there. There are swings, monkey bars, slides, and a merry-go-round at the neighborhood park, all promising her great fun. Since she knew no one in the area; at least, she knew how to mingle with a park. With her head held down and walking starry-eyed on the ground, she continued her saggy-faced blue-eyed journey. As she passed by each house, she wondered how such an area could lack the refreshing fun of freeze tag, or duck-duck-goose. She peeped between each crevice, and around every corner hunting for any sign of someone her age. She found no hope!

The park calmly awaited her arrival, as she painted her first footprint on the parks frail green grass. She went from the swings to the slide, from the slide to the merry-go-ride; but she found this time to be unfulfilling. She held the thought of leaving old friends to meet new ones. How could life be so gloomy? How could the transformation of going to new excitement turn melancholy? The little girl sat like a stone on the revolving merry-go-round, her legs positioned Indian style, and her eyes focused on a burette that she twiddled between her fingers. The ride slowly came to a halt. She decided to leave the park and head back to her new home.

With no friends to accept her and no knowledge of where to find any, all she could do was hope things would somehow get better. She noticed one thing as she was leaving the park. She trampled over colorful leaves she had either never seen, or never really paid any attention to. Her head bounced up from the ground, while her eyes squabbled up the tree from which the leaves fell. What appeared was a big beautiful tree filled with autumn love. The tree was draped with branches full of orangish, yellowish, greenish, and reddish leaves. Boy what a beautiful sight, she thought. How could a time so quiet, be filled with trees so loud? As a smile pricked her little round face, she skipped home having pushed aside any desolate feeling.

Sometimes the smallest stigmas speak volumes. Through the worst times, God has a way of getting our attention so that we acknowledge His presence. If it is but a candlestick in a dark house; even a candle has a way of radiating every place we carry it. God's natural creation served as a light for the little girl. She paid no mind to the seasons that had come and gone from birth, until a change occurred, and she needed to notice. Then, she noticed that the most beautiful creations come by way of nature. Though these creations are nature's participants, they are truly supernatural creations.

The only way full beauty maturates is by going through a process. Though it was but a tree for the girl, just like most people, she only noticed the *final* product. We never really witness the process someone, or something goes through. Just as the tree stood ground through changing seasons, we must do likewise. No one really knows what it took, or will take, for us to fulfill our destiny. Nevertheless, we must abide within our God.

Jesus chose one of the most superlative analogies to explicate what our relationship with Him should resemble. He likened it to a plant. In John 15, Jesus tells the disciples, He is the "vine" and we are the "branches." Through such analogy, Jesus demonstrates His command regarding our spiritual relationship. *A vine's purpose is to serve as a tool of nourishment.* The vine supports and provides for the branch. No matter how dry or worn out a vine looks externally; it is filled with sustaining nutrients. The internal strength helps the vine hold itself together and reproduce. The vine establishes such unique relationship with the branch; it becomes the sole supplier for the branch. As a matter of fact, the branches feed from the internal nourishment of the vine. The vine becomes connected to the branch through a *genuine commitment.* There is no way the vine will break its commitment to the branch.

The branches, on the other hand, play a much different role. Their job is to produce fruit, or leaves. The branches must have formal relationship with the vine in order to survive. They do one of two things. They either add beauty to the vine, or they lose face value. No one really pays much attention to the vine. People normally notice the glory of the branches; which is the fruit or beautiful leaves. People often say God does not need us. Based on the analogy Jesus left with us, I beg to differ. Without the branches the fruit is absent. God needs us to be reproductive of His glory. Genesis tells us we are made in the likeness of God. Just as the vine produces the branches, God wants us to produce fruit.

God needs us for His eternal purpose and glory. *"Even every one that is called by my name: for I have created him for my glory, I have formed him; yea, I have made him" (Isaiah 43:7).* The fruit accumulates glory toward the vine. The glory of the vine is what draws bystanders. The glory is what entices others to taste the fruit. There is one more additive, called, the *gardener.*

The gardener is the overseer of the whole process. The gardener knows *where* to plant, *how* to plant, in *what season* to plant, and *what seeds* to plant. He watches the progress between the vine and the branch. It is imperative that the gardener monitors the relationship between the two. The gardener knows the vine is going to do its job, because he planted the seed. He is the least bit worried about the vine. His true concern is amongst the branch and the fruit it bares.

When I was young, I had a friend that had a grape vineyard in his backyard. Three of my buddies, and I would travel six blocks up to his house. We designated one person as the watchdog. The others would sneak in his backyard to steal a bucket full of grapes, and run away. Some friends we were, huh! Man, those green grapes were sweet and delicious! I can taste them just telling you about them. I bet you can taste them too, huh! We did this at least three times a week, during the grape-growing season. Someone would pop the question, "Man, ya'll want to go get some grapes?" No verbal response was needed. A few times I remember seeing some old shriveled up, brownish looking grapes. They looked rotten. We left those behind. They got no love from us 'grape-thieves' (excuse my English). If we mistakenly grabbed some bad ones, whenever we got back to sort them, they were tossed out. Sometimes we would go to his house to visit him, and we were invited to eat the grapes. This is how we knew they had the plants in the first place. Watch who you allow to visit you! (Sorry for the diversion—that should be in another book!)

My friend's dad would cut away certain branches and throw them out. His dad played the role of a gardener. It was his duty to cut away those branches that were not producing, to free the others from any contamination. He also clipped the ends of others in order to provoke them to develop more fruit. Weeks later the very area he clipped away had bloomed beautiful grapes. At times the branches can get too comfortable. The branches have found a comfort zone when the amount of production does not change. To quicken the branches progress the gardener moves the vine from its comfort zone to another place. His dad was also, the *overseer*. Can you imagine being a branch that is constantly being cut on all the time? Or, being placed in one area only to be moved from that area to be re-established elsewhere, all for your growth? How similar our life!

Excess Fat

God is our gardener, Jesus is the vine, and we are the branches. How many times have we lost a job, lost a child, gotten lied on, ridiculed, ostracized, saw someone else receive a promotion we felt was ours, gotten over-looked, had to eat leftovers daily, went without food, etc.? God was only cutting away the *excess fat*. The Gardener was pruning us. God allows certain things to occur to draw us closer to Him. He wants to know just how much we trust Him. Are your children more important to you than God? Has your job caused you to commit idolatry? Does your "friend" of the opposite sex over step boundaries that demean your God-ordained spouse? Can hunger pains for something else separate you from His love? How important is God to you? As stated in the earlier chapter, we have to learn how to live *balanced*. God allows painful situations to occur to test our faith. He also allows situations to shape us into better people. We have to be shaped into what God desires for us to become. I often tell people "We can't be too *earthly* where God can't use us, and we can't think we're too *holy* where people don't want to bother with us."

It is true that we should not worry about what people think about our walk. Thus, this remains concrete only if their determination toward us will cause our separation from God. People have a demeaning way to say things that will make us reevaluate our decision to walk with God. It is one thing to separate from the "Christian critics." It is another thing to separate from people who want God, because we feel like our Christianity promotes us above them.

One of God's Levitical laws, in Leviticus 18, was for us to "love our neighbors as ourselves." Jesus echoed the same commandment in John 15:12. This commandment promotes desegregation with others. We, as Christians, are no better than the next person. As a Christian, we are required to be a light to the non-Christians that are in the dark, *Ye are the light of the world" (Matthew 5:14)*. The glory of God that is alive within us should entice all bystanders. People should look upon us and desire a taste of God's gleaming glory and godly love should draw men to God's Kingdom, and not push those who seriously want God away. We never know who God is working on. Therefore, God commands us to love everyone as ourselves.

Any hatred we may have can blow a person's

dwindling light out. A person that is on the brink of believing in God can be totally sidetracked by our actions. No one wants to be a part of our Christian faith, if our definition of Christianity represents hell. Christianity is a daily process. Therefore God cuts, clips, and shaves to make us better representatives. We may lose precious gems along the way. The loss of those gems are purposed to deepen our trust in God. God does not prune us, or shift us from one place to another to hurt us. He does it for our production. We need to produce fruit, fruit, and more fruit. So He clips those old shriveled grapes: trimming the excess fat to help develop us, cutting away the stuff that is unhealthy for our lives and unhealthy looking.

One of the most amazing things about God is we cannot depict the spirit of God in our natural mind. Jesus used the analogy of the vine and the branch to symbolize His relationship with His children. To understand the true meaning of this analogy will take a deep spiritual revelation. Since you may not be familiar with a vine, lets use an apple tree for the sake of this illustration.

The *end* result of an apple tree is beautiful. It looks healthy, and promising. It is full of lovely green leaves, and beautiful red apples. If we were to stand back and gaze upon a mature apple tree, we would notice the pleasant view it exhibits. The view will make it worth our precious time.

To just quickly look at it, then run, pick a few apples, and leave, would almost be an insult to the apple tree. Why? Because it is like taking the tree for granted. Unless we are the actual gardener, or in this case the caregiver of the apple tree, we may never notice the growth process the tree endured to produce.

The apple tree paid a price to birth beautiful red apples. We only pay attention to the end result. We often look past the ice-cold winters, the broken branches incurred, the branches lost, the seasonal draughts, and the sawing off of branches, the tree must have endured. *According to the N.C.S.U. College of Agriculture, "Proper training and pruning will develop strong frame work and help yield high fruit production. Improperly trained fruit trees, usually, mean weak limbs which could result in fruit breakage under heavy fruit loads."* We also by-pass the years of growth from the time the apple seed was planted, and the ground being cultivated to present itself with glorious red fruit. We do not watch the growth stages. The only changes we may notice; over the course of time, are the height and changes in leaves.

The growth of the vine and branch are the same; likewise, man with God. God uses *external things to affect our internal growth.* Yeah, you can quote the Bible, but is your relationship with God improving? Is God getting glory out of your life? God does not illuminate man to allow us perception of what is happening inside the man. Man cannot see spiritual growth through his natural eye. Man must see spiritual growth through *spiritual senses.*

Spiritual growth is an invisible growth. We never notice spiritual growth until it is revealed to us. Spiritual growth is similar to the growth of the apple tree. We can observe a tree for years, and only know it as a tree. We never notice an apple tree is an apple tree until it is revealed unto us. Either the one who planted the seed must tell us, or time must reveal it. Time reveals an apple tree through the appearance of *apples.*

God planted you here. *"Before I formed thee in the belly I knew thee; and before thou camest forth out of the womb I sanctified thee, and I ordained thee a prophet unto the nations" (Jeremiah 1:5).* God explicates His compassion for us. He says before we had a mind He knew us. Though people said we were a mistake, we were on His mind. God planted us here. That speaks for itself. Someone may have said that they did not plan us, and said we were a mistake. If they did not plan us . . .*someone* did. Who else could have planned us if it was not God? God just used our mom and dad to manifest us in the flesh. Either God will reveal to others we are His child by speaking to them, or He allows time to reveal His children. Time reveals an apple tree through the glory of beautiful red apples. *Time reveals a child of God through their walk, talk, deeds, and actions.*

Gardening for Glory

It is easy for a human to walk by a vine holding beautiful green or red grapes, and salivate for them. Things of the flesh (meaning natural appearance) draw the flesh. What do I mean? The grapes are easy to grasp, because we can see them through our natural eye. We can see the natural green glory of a grape that appeals to our sight. The grape's appearance causes a gravitational pull from our natural man toward that which is naturally appealing to us. We have been schooled on grapes. Therefore we move toward the grapes by *nature.*

The spirit of God is the same. Once our spiritual senses are trained, they are drawn like a magnet to things of the *spirit.* The glory of God within us generates a magnetic pull from others toward us. We will not know why people are drawn to us; it will not be because of our appearance. It is the appearance of a grape or leaf that draws us to the plant. *It is the inner being of a man that draws others to that man.* The most amazing feat is it looks like gravitation to that particular man. The reality is it is *God* inside that man drawing people unto *Himself.* God said in II Corinthians 6:16 that we are "His temple and He would dwell in us; walk in us, and be our God." He also said, *"And I, if I be lifted up from the earth, will draw all men unto me" (John 12:32).* He is using us for His glory.

God's glory within a person draws others in order to build His Kingdom. He uses us to grab hold of those that are lost. That is why our relationship with God is extremely important. If the grape vine were filled with those brown shriveled up grapes, no one would desire a taste. People would refrain from moving toward the tree. If we are constantly cursing, lying, fornicating, stealing, and gossiping as a Christian; then people will eventually refrain from being around us. We understand Christianity is a process, and no one is perfect. Many times that is just a mask people wear to escape changing bad ways. They boast about being a "Christian," but the fruit they produce is old, shriveled habits. Instead of pulling people toward them, they confuse the lost and push away believers.

God's glory also has the ability to entice believers. The glory within the believer is similar to the gravitational pull toward the holy city that is discussed in Chapter two of this book. When God's glory begins to manifest itself from within the believer, people automatically become fond of that believer. God's favor is a component of His glory. This is why people have a misunderstanding with why certain people receive so much attention from others. People get jealous of a person with God's favor. They misunderstand favored people, because they misunderstand God.

Sometimes, people will tell us they do not know why they hold such resentment toward a person. One reason they do not understand the favor over a person's life; or the resentment they hold toward that person with God's favor is because they are trying to understand that person in their *flesh* (carnalities). *Natural beings cannot comprehend supernatural* things. It is not the people misunderstanding the resentment they hold toward favored believers; it is the enemy within, warring against the God in those favored people. They do not understand the enemy using them to war against God's favored. Anytime God uses us to help establish His Kingdom, the enemy will try to use people to attack us: especially if we are doing a good job.

This is why disconnecting from the enemy by getting closer to God is critical. The God in you knows the God in me, because He is the same God. The Holy Spirit will reveal to us God's people. Therefore, we will not have any time or room to dislike His own. The spirit will convict us of jealousy, envy, or strife against our brother or sister. *"But the Comforter, which is the Holy Ghost, whom the Father will send in my name, he shall teach you all things, and bring all things to your remembrance, whatsoever I have said unto you" (John 14:26).* God will teach us how to love and remind us that He commanded us to love in spite of the odds. Godly love will override and rule out jealousy. It will make us repent for allowing the enemy use us to hate another brother, or gossip about a sister. It is all a part of growing pains. It is a part of God shaving the excess fat off for His glory.

Romantic Devoir

The analogy of the vine and the branch is a romantic commitment. The vine and the branch are so involved with each other nothing can interrupt the process of producing fruit. As slated earlier, the vine is totally committed to the branch. There is no possibility of the vine annulling its commitment. It almost resembles two new lovers so into each other, they become blinded by everything except their romantic involvement with one another. The vine is committed to satisfying the branch through its ability to impregnate it by pumping nutrients to nourish, build, and strengthen it. The branch displays its love by sacrificing itself to become impregnated by the vine's nutrients in order to produce ripe fruit.

An abiding branch understands its commitment to the vine will not only benefit itself, but the *plant* as a whole. They are almost in conversation with each other on a constant basis:

Vine: "Stay with me."
Branch: "I will stay."
Vine: "It will be okay, I know the situation looks dim."
Branch: "It is too hard, the pain is too severe."
Vine: "I know I'm immensely touched by your pain; stay strong."
Branch: "How much longer must I go through this?"
Vine: "It will all work together for your good. Hang in there. I need you to hang in there."
Branch: "I believe in you, I trust in you."
Vine: "Be strong, and of good courage."
Branch: "I'm holding on. You brought me through the last crisis. I'm holding on. How could he (the Gardener) tolerate me losing and going through so much?"
Vine: "Hold on to your faith. He is building you."
Branch: "I'm quitting, I'm giving up."

Vine: "No, you are not, I can't afford to lose you. You must abide in me. Hold on! Your strength will help others."

It is almost as if the vine constantly tries to persuade the branch of their commitment to one another. The vine endures the struggle with the branch, and becomes the strength during a weak time. It tries to comfort the branch. It tries to secure the branch's feeling. Through the conversation, we never hear the vine talk about dropping the branch. The vine constantly instructs the branch to stay, to hold on, and to be encouraged. The vine displays stability in their relationship. It pays to be in a relationship we can totally depend on. This is what the branch has with the vine. The branch has a relationship with the vine it can totally trust.

For the branch to remain in touch with the vine, it has to love the vine. The pain ridden situations of constantly being cut, transposed, reshaped, molded, and clipped must be overshadowed by the branch's love for its maker. The branch's love for the vine keeps its faith in the vine operative. Some branches wither, give up, and die. Others remain faithful, full of love, and fight to remain alive. They fight because they can see the big picture. They see the promise being fulfilled, through their belief in that given promise. They also see themselves overcoming labor pains in order to produce their promise. The branch can see the promise being fulfilled before it is manifested.

Apostle Paul wrote to the church of Corinth in I Corinthians 13:13 that amongst faith, hope, and charity: charity prevails. Charity, of course, is interchanged for the word—love. Without the branches' love is there no relationship? Through the entire trauma that appears, the relationship will die if the branch does not have enough love for the vine.

God gave me two different unique sets of grandparents. One set—I do not know how long they have been married; the other set have been married for over fifty years. I can see them deeply grounded in love through the stages of boyfriend/girlfriend. I can see granddaddy-courting grandmamma through the park like he owned the place. I can see him pushing her on the swing with a grin that will make the blues smile. I can see them elated with joy through months of their engagement, even through the first tenth of what is now a fifty-year marriage.

I likened their relationship to common relationships. There comes a day when we get tired and fall out of love. How can a couple remain together for so long; better yet remain married? Relationships require us to go through different battles with one another. Relationships go through arguments, disagreements, name-calling, relationship re-evaluations, and repenting for making the agreement to be in the relationship. There comes a time where we just do not feel like we love our companion the same. The key is—genuine love is not based on what *we feel.* Our feelings sway us; they will take us all over the place. I have come to realize that my grandparents understood the big picture of their relationship. They knew they had an agreement to remain committed no matter what occurred. They hold faith and trust in one another. Their love is not solely based on feelings; therefore, they have the ability to survive their battles.

The branch must be in-tune with the vine enough to see the big picture. The branch's love must drown out any selfish desires, and it must reciprocate the vine's love. Their love for one another cannot be one sided. If the branch becomes selfish it will lose focus, dry out, and die.

The vine loves the branch so much; it only requires the branch to withstand the times. The vine empowers the branch to endure and produce. It believes in the branch it produced. The branch must love the vine enough to believe it can withstand the times within the vine. The branch must also believe that the promise it was presented is secure.

The Gardener prunes us to shine bright and help make a difference for others of the world. We go through battles as an exemplary standard for others. We also go through tests to be an encouragement for others, and help them make it through their own battles. Develop enough faith in God to remain committed through your most painful situations.

Practical Principles

Hebrew 12:6

"For whom the Lord loveth He chasteneth, and scourgeth every son whom He receives."

Don't think that everything you go through is the enemy. Sometimes we give the devil too much credit.

Hopefully, you did not go through life without being disciplined. Can you remember being whipped for doing something wrong? My parents used to explain to me that they whipped me, not because they liked to do it, but because they loved me. They had a responsibility to correct me as their child. This is what God does. He corrects us as His children. He has to correct us to keep us from getting into the wrong situations. His desire is for us to be the best we can be. If He did not love us, He would not care enough to correct us.

Philippians 4:13

*"I can do all things through Christ
which strengtheneth me."*

Through the toughest times we have to dig deep inside ourselves to make it to the end. Whatever it is that hinders you from becoming a success, you must dig deep inside you to overcome the test. Have you ever tried to run in a pool against the pool's natural flow? It is not easy. Through your determination not to be defeated by what is natural, you dig deep inside yourself for strength to run against the flow of the pool. There is a rich spirit inside you that will help you reach all of your goals.

When life bombards us with obstacles that wear us weary, we must draw from God's supernatural strength to help us run against life's natural flow. We can do all things through Christ, and let nothing tell us differently.

Summary Prayer

Lord. I am sorry for all the wrong I have done. I know that You don't chasten me without having a logical reason. I apologize for my sins. Please forgive me, God. I really love You. I know I have done wrong. I never meant to hurt You.

Give me the strength, God to overcome and to accomplish the things that You have set before me. When life wages war against me, provide me Your strength. I trust in You for everything. You are my God, my shield, and my strength. Thank you, God, for your reigning power!

Chapter 7

Kingdom Building

What an extraordinary analogy; the vine and the branch! Jesus is a man of such wisdom; He chose an analogy that contains multiple messages. This analogy also represents *Kingdom building.*

It amazes me that one vine contains enough power to supply multiple branches. It really does not matter how many branches are produced—what really matters is that they all belong to *one* vine. The vine contains enough nutrition within itself to transfer into each branch what they need to survive. Each time a branch is clipped, it continues to extract from the vine what it needs for re-growth. As long as the branch is *abiding,* the nutrients have a free-flowing tunnel. If the branch gets disconnected, the supply chain is disconnected.

A most mind-boggling phenomenon is the vine's ability to disperse a quality amount of nutrients to each branch. Every branch that is attached to the vine presents itself an opportunity to partake of the vine's nutrients. Each branch has equal opportunity. If a branch at the bottom dies and the one at the top lives, it is not because the vine ran out of supplements.

Can you picture a vine or tree decorated with multiple branches? It seems like the branch at the bottom would receive more nutrient because it is the closest to the root—closest to the foundation. It seems like it has first dibs to how much and how often it desires to partake from the vine. This is not so. The truth of the matter is, each branch has a chance to extract from the vine exactly what it needs to grow; the branch at the top, as much as the branch at the bottom.

Just because the branch at the bottom is the first to grow from the vine, does not mean it will inherit special benefits. People will not rush toward it because it looks like it is the closest to the root, nor does it mean it will be the most productive. Whichever branch sprouts the most fruit/glory is the one that will entice the most outsiders toward it. The branch can be the closest to the bottom, in the middle, or at the very top. The vine is most interested in encouraging each attached branch to produce. Therefore, it dispenses nutrients on a constant basis for each branch.

The vine's task is to impart into everything that is attached to it. If a branch dies it will not be because it was not receiving what it needed to survive. Think about it. Why would a branch in the middle die, but the one at the top live? Could it be because the vine ceased to supply in the middle? Or, that the vine rejected the middle and skipped over it to provide to the top? God forbid! The vine is established throughout the whole tree. No matter where we find a branch, there is a vine supporting it. From the bottom to the top of the tree, we will find the vine; from the vine, a branch appears.

The vine establishes itself through the whole plant, sort of like a millipede. We are able to see the whole body of the millipede, with multiple legs attached to her body. Wherever her body stops growth the legs stop appearing. There is no way the vine can skip over itself to produce in another area. For the vine to skip a branch would signify breakage somewhere in the vine. This is impossible for the vine. Wherever the vine stops growing the branches stop appearing.

This is the way God made the vine. God orchestrated everything in the vine/branch relationship to be founded on the vine. Nothing can work without the vine, nor be produced without the vine: no branches, no leaves, and no fruit. The vine plays the most imperative role in the relationship.

So Jesus instructs us in John 15 to *abide* in Him as He *abides* in us. This command is an interchangeable command. How can we live in something while that something is living in us? The vine and branch become so involved with each other they began to look like one another. If no one ever told us that the branch was a branch, we would probably think the vine was the whole plant. The vine and branch all begin to look like one; as a whole. Jesus wants to establish a relationship with us that is so strong that people cannot sever His spiritual being from ours. When people see you, they see Him.

In looking at the vine/branch relationship, I have noticed their relationship is built through the invisible. The relational growth is predicated on what is happening inside the two. The transformation of a developing branch, the branch growing strong, and producing fruit is based on internal growth. We cannot really see the nutrients or supplements being transposed from the vine to the branch. We just believe in what is there, what is happening, and what is expected to happen. The growth of the plant confirms the validity of our faith in the invisible to manifest visibly. As the plant grows it confirms what we believe. The internal supplements help to transform the branch externally. They help mold the appearance of the plant. The glory we see *outwardly* is a direct result of an *inward* work.

There are natural laws that connote the growth of a fruit tree. The fact that natural laws already confirm this growth process negates our faith in a natural tree's growth. This illustration is only relevant to help us understand what our relationship with God should resemble. Our faith for spiritual growth in God is imperative.

Internal Cleansing by the Spoken Word

The question is, "How can we live in something while that something is living in us?" What a perplexing question? It seems like an impossibility to live *in* something at the same time it is living *in* us. This question almost has family ties to other intricate questions that are impossible to answer; like why God is God; how is He God; how did He become God; how does He do what He does, or *why* does He do it the way He does it? These are open-ended questions that teachers, theologians, doctors, or computers have no closing answers to. We are not apt to figure out why godliness is what it is. Paul wrote in his letter to Timothy "godliness is a mystery." God is God; and His ways, teachings, and commandments are true.

Is it really possible to live in something while that something is living in us?

What Jesus commands us to do is abide in Him as He abides in us. He asks us to live, or remain in Him as He lives/remains in us. It is written in John 1, that in the "beginning was the Word," the "Word was God," was with God, and the "Word became flesh." *My* physical body cannot live inside *your* physical body. Since Jesus cannot dwell in us physically, He must dwell in us spiritually. Jesus is considered the spoken Word. We cannot know Jesus without knowing His Word, and we cannot know God without knowing His Son.

When God said, "Let there be light," (Genesis chapter 1), we would not have literally seen the words He spoke. We would have only seen the *manifestation* of what He spoke. We would have seen the *result* of the spoken Word—the appearance of light. Spoken words are spirit. We cannot see words floating through the air when they are spoken. We see either the words manifested on paper, or the manifestation of what was spoken. Anything that God spoke, was manifested by-way tangible Jesus. Without Jesus no word can become tangible. This is not said to limit God's unlimited capabilities. He just uses a, for the lack of better words, facet of His Triune Being to manifest the intangible to the tangible. We cannot see God. We would have been able to see Jesus—Jesus is tangible, God is intangible, but both Jesus and God are the same.

What God spoke was taken by His holy prophets and written down as biblical memorials, and current applications. The Bible is a blue print for how we should develop and live our lives. It is the instructional print-out of how to put ourselves together. What God spoke was manifested on paper for us to eat.

We, as children of God, must eat what has been recorded in the Bible. How do we *eat the Bible?* We eat it through the spirit of God that dwells in us, by reading and studying the scriptures. As we study and read, our spiritual man becomes more developed. It begins to harmonize with the things of God, and God Himself. Our flesh (carnalities), does not comprehend this, because we are talking about something that benefits us spiritually, not carnally. Yet, the Bible helps us control our flesh by walking in the spirit. *"This I say then, walk in the Spirit, and ye shall not fulfill the lust of the flesh" (Galatians 5:16).* Romans 8 provides information about our spirituality versus our flesh (carnalities). It tells us our spirit and carnal-ities do not get along. They *war* against each other.

Jesus told the devil when He was being tempted on the mount, *"Man shall not live by bread alone, but by every word that proceedeth out of the mouth of God" (Matthew 4:4).* Our Bible is a part of the mouth of God. Everything written in our Bible is the spoken Word from God. *"All scripture is give by inspiration of God, and is profitable for doctrine, for reproof, for correction, for instruction in righteous-ness:" (2 Timothy 3:16).* The simple fact that Jesus rebutted the devil's offer for food with the Word of God, denotes that our Bible is our *spiritual* food. Jesus counteracted the enemy's offer for carnal food with a "spiritual food" revelation.

It is evident Jesus was hungry, but He did not act on His fleshly desires. You ask me how do I know Jesus was hungry? I know He was hungry because the enemy will always try to attack us through what he thinks are our vulnerabilities. Jesus was without food for forty days and forty nights, and the Bible clearly says after Jesus *fasted*—He was hungry. If Jesus were under the influence of His flesh, He would have turned the stone into bread, as the enemy requested. Galatians 5:16 tell us if we "walk in the spirit we will not fulfill the flesh." Jesus was, obviously, acting through the Spirit. Therefore, He was able to reject the flesh to embrace a spiritually based truth. *"Man shall not live by bread alone but by every word that proceedeth out of the mouth of God."*

We shall live then by the Word that comes from

God's mouth: the Bible. Romans 8 says to be "carnally minded is death," but to be "spiritually minded is life and peace." God is spiritual. Based on Jesus' reply to the devil (He answered with the Word of God), we have learned that any Word from the mouth of God is *life*. Tangible food could not help Jesus live eternally. Accepting the enemy's offer would have only corrupted Jesus' destiny; or rather, God's plan.

The Bible is our tangible Word used to feed our spirit. Jesus said we shall *live* by God's Word. We eat carnal food to physically remain alive, we must eat spiritual food to remain spiritually alive; nevertheless, spiritual food helps us live our physical lives wisely.

As we eat (feast on) the Bible, we will learn different spiritual interactions. We will learn interactions like faith in God, hope in God, love in God, prayer, praise, and worshiping God. We will become more familiar with Jesus as we become more active with the Word of God. We will learn of Him and become more in-tune with Him. When we learn about Jesus, we learn about God (John 14:7).

After Jesus commanded us to abide in Him, He then says in John 15:3 that we are *cleansed* through the Words He spoke. Jesus tells us that taking heed to His Word is a cleansing agent. It is somewhat like filling a washing machine full of stained white clothing.

If we turn on the washing machine without detergent, when the cycle finishes we will *still* have stained white clothing. If we fill the machine with detergent and turn on the machine, the addition of a detergent helps cleanse the white clothing. Eating God's word while abiding in Him, adds the *detergent* to our body. The battles we suffer take us through the cycles necessary to cleanse us. This is why eating the Word is important.

I told you John declared that the Word became flesh. This manifestation of the Word becoming flesh is known as—Jesus. So when we eat the Word we are eating, or partaking of Jesus (and all He is), and yes, even God Himself.

While Paul was teaching the church at Ephesus how to conduct a marriage, he metaphorically compared a marriage to Christ's love for the church. Then he said Christ gave Himself for the church *"That he might sanctify and cleanse it with the washing of water by the word," (Ephesians 5:26). "* What I want you to focus on is the fact that Christ died for the church to *reconcile* and *cleanse* it. We are a part of the church in a spiritual sense. Of course, Christ did not die for the church building down the street from our home. He died for His people, His creation; which includes you and me. The Ephesians Scripture, says He cleanses His *church;* or *you and me,* by the washing of the Word.

So as His Word fills our eyes, slithers down our eye sockets, stampedes our mind, falls down our inner being, and knocks on the door of our soul; we are welcoming in Jesus. When Jesus comes to the party—things happen. People's lives begin to change. Wedding water is turned into wine, dead men rise, deaf men start hearing, and the blind recover their sight when Jesus arrives. (These are some of the miracles Jesus performed during His ministry). Jesus makes an appearance because He cares enough about us to change some things within us. This is why God performs miracles, for the purpose of enticing our mind. He wants us to believe He is the only answer. Yet, God wants us to believe in who He is. He wants us to know that He truly loves us.

Once we give birth to believing in God, He has us exactly where He wants us. Once we welcome Him into the doors of our soul, He anchors us to stay in the fight. He prunes something in our life through every battle we overcome. While we are fighting a battle, He just might be scrubbing away a quick temper we may have. Once the battle is over, we will find ourselves with some meekness. He will scrub away the hate inside us, until He can see love. God enters to scrub away the dirty build up.

We have to eat the Word with a heart of commitment toward the laws, statutes, and ordinances of God. As we conduct ourselves accordingly, we begin to dwell in Jesus through our commitment to His spoken Word. We have to get to where we love studying and reading the Word of God. Just like the analogy of the vine and branches, we have to fall so deeply in love with God that His desires become *our* desires. We have to trust in His lead. Amid the pruning, trials, and tribulations, we must stay focused on the goal. Jesus, unceasingly, supplies us with nutrients while we are connected to Him.

It is critical to keep our pipes clear during this process. Pipe blockage occurs when we lose focus and become disconnected. Jesus will always remain stable. Jesus is so self-assured; He knows our abiding in Him will greatly benefit us. He is the flowing electricity in an electrical socket. We will never get proper results, without plugging into Him. He makes it opportune for us to partake of the nutrients inside Him whenever we need them. God said, *"Out of your belly shall flow rivers of living waters" (John 7:38)*. Whenever we are in need God has given us permission to draw from His well.

Who Jesus is in our lives will determine *how* He abides in us. When our ways become His ways, we begin the process of interchanging relationships. Think of it like putting on a glove. When we put on a glove, it takes the formation of our hand. The glove is already created in the image of our hand. We are the one desiring to cover our hand with the glove. Once we put it on, we control what it does. This is the relationship, God wants with us. God created us in His image (Genesis 1:16). Much like a glove, He desires to pull us back over the image He created us in. He desires to pull us over Himself. Once we allow Him to pull us over Him, He is able to dance inside us.

This is how we live in something while that something is living inside of us. We abide in Jesus by allowing Him to set boundaries over our thoughts, our speech, and our actions. What we are doing externally is a derivative of what is happening internally.

We know it is what is inside the glove that causes it to react the way it does. God wants a similar relationship with us. He does not want to manipulate and control us. He knows the directions we must take to be productive.

When we are abiding in Him, God is able to direct our path (Proverbs 3:6). We are in Jesus. As we grow in the Word, He grows in our heart. While we are living inside Jesus, Jesus is living inside us. Jesus does not live in us physically, but He lives in our heart. We cannot cut our body down the center and find the Word, but the Word lives in our hearts. God dwells in us because He is a Spirit (John 4:24). The Word in us is Spirit. The God in us is contains the Word in us, and God's Spirit, through Jesus, teaches us and reminds us what we have been taught (John 14:26). Our interaction with a Triune God systematically cleanses us.

Made for His Purpose

The whole concept of the abiding process is formulated to teach us how to have faith, and how to love regardless of the circumstance. I talked earlier about the uncomprehending ways of life. Life throws multiple curve balls our way. At sometime, we must learn when and how to swing the bat. Jesus gives us vital instructions that lay stable foundations for building a quality home. If we miss these instructions, we will miss the most important part of the construction process. He simply says to "abide in Him."

As we go through the process required for us to

learn how to abide, we begin laying bricks and adding mortar to the foundation. God allows life to help shape and mold us. We must stay in Him while going through this process. Allow God to scrub away the build-up, and cut away the excess fat. Every time life boulders over us, we have to get up and extract from God what we need to survive. We must hold onto our faith through the pruning process. If we lose our faith and our hope, our pipeline will clog up and rust. If we keep our faith pipe open, we will continue to receive God's reviving nutrition. The more we grow in God, the more we will learn of God's sovereignty.

His reign over our life is what provokes us to *tell somebody.* There is no way a person can dwell in the sewer of sin, be saved by God's sovereign power, and not want someone to *know* about their transformation. Nor can a person be delayed deliverance from the nastiness of life, finally receive deliverance and *not* have a testimony. If someone lives in a stinking sewer long enough, once they find a better smelling place they will make *sure* someone knows what they were delivered from.

The glory painted over our life is not only for our benefit. It is for the benefit of adding more believers into His established Kingdom. Jesus says, abide in Him, and learn what He needs to teach us. Once He teaches us, He will send us out to help recruit more branches. He will use us to produce fruit to benefit the Kingdom (John 15:16). To be dead in Jesus is unacceptable. He says every branch that does not produce is taken away (John 15:2). God chooses us and teaches us to speak highly of Him to others. Once we present Christ to another person, their transformation process starts. It starts because we have disseminated godly seeds within them, *"So then faith cometh by hearing, and hearing by the word of God" (Romans 10:17).* When a person accepts us, they accept God. Hence, we have helped reconciliate another branch into the Kingdom. This is why the proverb says, *"The fruit of the righteous is a tree of life: and he that winneth souls is wise" (Proverbs 11:30).*

Jesus presented Himself with all rights reserved for the benefit of God's Kingdom. He walked this earth, was persecuted, hated, and crucified—with us on His mind. The abiding process is purposed for us to learn how to die to ourselves, and live for others. We have to learn just as Jesus learned. Yet, He gives us the benefit of not enduring physical wounds of impounding nails as He did on the cross. God does not want to take away our fun. He wants to show us how to have fun, inner peace, and joy at the same time. He says, *"Greater love hath no man than this, that a man lay down his life for his friend" (John 3:16).* He teaches us this same principle: first through *scripture,* second through our *life.* The best ministry a person has is through their walk with God. When multiple people witness us struggle in life, and see us continue to worship God in ministry.

We need to reserve some of our selfish rights and lay down our life for some friends. He asked us to love one another. There is no greater love than to:

"lay down" our life for our mother.

"lay down clubbing" for a drug-infested brother.

Why not "lay down" or give up fornication to help save a wayward sister? Or, even their friends?

What about the people that we do not see watching us who admire us so much?

This is what Kingdom building is all about. It is about allowing God to use us as His chosen vessels to save a lost soul. It is about an abounding love that penetrates barriers to reconcile God's people.

The next life we touch may be the one who has death wishes written all over it. We may be the one who can show them the way before their time runs out. Our abiding growth may be the example they need to change for "Kingdom purposes."

Perhaps it could be *you.* You may be the person that, somehow, keeps escaping danger. This book may be the last opportunity you get to change for the best. You could make a decision that will change the destiny of your life. God keeps sparing you, and you know it. You know it has been a supernatural power that helped you escape destruction. You may not witness God's grace the next time.

Maybe you keep backsliding. You tamper with holy things, and then you turn around and fiddle with sinful things. You know God convicts you every time you touch "that" sin. Whenever you decide to take heed to the Spirit and be an over-comer, your witness will become enormously more effective.

Nothing we have accomplished in life has surprised God, and our shortcomings in life have not shocked Him. God knows all about us. He designed and created us. The most disturbing factor in life is to have someone try to "pull something over on us." To see someone do wrong, then come to us feigning a state of innocence is most disturbing.

How can we function correctly living an untruthful life? If it disturbs us to see someone we are not fond of put on a facade, how much more, our friend and Lord? Think of how God feels to see His children play the harlot, then pray for blessings? Think about how it makes "Daddy" feel to see His unique creation curse their brother and bless Him (God)?

For God to know that He made us for His purpose and see us portray the son of the enemy must be highly distressing. The enemy comes to "kill, steal, and destroy." What a delight for the enemy to use God's children to defame and belittle their kindred. The enemy loves an unfruitful witness. He tricks them to believe it is okay to say they love God and keep old habits.

It is not okay to be lukewarm in a lukewarm generation. When a person is lukewarm their witness is affected, their fruit is affected, their life is affected, the people surrounding them are affected, and God is affected (Revelations 3).

Once we understand that we are made for His purpose our actions will cause us to supernaturally line up according to God's will (Ephesians 1:11). It takes effort on our part, but God is willing to do the rest.

The End Result

It is refreshing to walk in a well-maintained park during a mild spring day. The glory of God's natural creation has the ability to captivate us; just as it did the little girl, mentioned in a previous chapter who noticed nature's own, while heading back to her new home.

Have you ever noticed a full-grown tree? Have you ever looked upon a huge tree that shed different color leaves onto beautiful green grass?

It is common to notice a neatly painted apple tree inside a pre-school reading book. Somewhere in the book we might see a nicely shaped apple, with dark green colored leaves, and rich brown painted branches. Sometimes, this beautiful tree dwells somewhere along the paths of a neatly painted hill.

The tree usually has bright red apples hanging from it. Though I have taken a journey through a preschool book, the book only mirrors images of Mother Nature. We may not see a picture of such in every part of the world, but it is a picture of truth.

Sometimes, I travel down the southern Texas highways or up through the northeastern U.S. hemisphere. I have noticed there is beautiful greenery sitting alongside the highways the farther south I drive down Texas, or the farther north I drive through Tennessee. There are big dark green painted trees, and miles full of dark green grass living beside the road. I never realized how beautiful a tree could be.

We often overlook nature, much like, the little

girl did. It may take growing old in age, or isolated loneliness to really notice nature's beauty.

The more I fathom the beauty of those trees, the more I understand the harmony of the total tree. I can see those beautiful green leaves that are born from those long brown branches. I also see those brown branches that spring from the tree trunk. When I think about that huge tree trunk, I wonder about those stable roots that are buried inside rich soil. Every part of the tree plays a significant role to produce a beautiful tree.

It is only my thoughts that glamorize every part of the tree. As previously stated, we only notice what *attracts* us. We do not pay much attention to the tree's body frame—the trunk, the unseen roots. We see those beautiful green leaves, and the fruit the tree may bear. We focus on the end result.

Proverbs 11:28b says, "But the righteous shall flourish as a branch." After we have learned how to abide in Jesus, commune with Jesus, trust in Jesus, and allow Jesus to cleanse us; then we are ready to flourish. *Webster's New Student Dictionary* says to "flourish" means to *thrive*. It means to achieve success, prosper, and to grow luxuriantly. Our relationship with God through Jesus is for our benefit.

We want to run right after we are born. There is no way a newborn baby will jump out of the incubator to run back to the delivery room to momma. It is a step-by-step process. It takes time and effort for the baby to learn how to run. The baby has to learn how to roll over to her knees, she has to learn how to crawl, she must learn how to walk, and then she can run. As it is in a life, so it is in this Christian walk.

We have to learn how to build a relationship with God through Jesus. We have to learn how to allow God to cleanse us, mold us, and build us. God takes us through a step-by-step process. The process all begins with our faith. People talk about Christianity like it is some cakewalk. This is definitely no cakewalk. It takes courage, perseverance, and determination. What we are doing in Christianity is stepping out of the old, and stepping into the new. *"Therefore if any man be in Christ, he is a new creature: old things are passed away; behold, all things are become new" (II Corinthians 5:17).*

It is similar to Clark Kent.

Clark Kent was a normal man that had a higher calling to help others. He would go into a phone booth and come out as Superman. Clark Kent was natural, and Superman was supernatural. He stepped out of the old man and into the new man.

We are constantly learning how to live righteous. Our mind should be continuously changing (if you are serious about resembling God). The Apostle Paul said we are to be, *"Transformed by the renewing or our mind" (Romans 12:2).* We learn how to live righteous through the process of mental and spiritual transformation. Righteous simply means right standing. It means to be standing right with God (re-read what I've just said to you). Let me ask you a question that will help you see the revelation. God just asked me, "Who are you standing with?" My reply is, "I am going to stand right with you." Let me put it like this to make sure you got it.

A mother might tell her son, "Dee, stand right over there until I get back!" Dee's mother established a place for him to stand. She has mental landmarks where her son should be standing when she returns. When she comes back she knows her son should be standing right with, or next to, those landmarks.

Now we know "righteous" means to stand right with God, or to stand right next to Him! If we find ourselves in His presence we would "literally" be afraid to do anything unpleasing in His sight. We have to look at it like our parents are standing next to us. Would we fornicate in the same room with our mother? I don't think so. Therefore, *right-standing* means that God is in the same area we are in no matter where we are.

So the proverb says, *"The righteous shall flourish as a branch."* Just as those big trees bloomed in beauty, we as righteous children of God's shall do the same. If we are standing right next to Him, we will have no choice but to achieve success. There is no way we can stand in God's presence, without first dying to ourselves. To die to ourselves means to let go of things that are unpleasing to God. To stand in His presence also means that we will resemble who He is. God is success. God is production. God is luxurious.

Moses stood in the presence of God and communed with Him on Mount Sinai. When he returned to the Israelites with God's instructions, they were afraid to look upon Moses because his face was shining from being in the very presence of God. He wore a veil when he spoke God's words to the people. He did not know that the veil was not covering his whole face once he returned. The interaction of being in God's presence was manifested by the appearance of Moses' face. This is what the people saw when the veil was removed from Moses' face; they saw the *appearance* of God.

The Israelites were afraid to look at God. They knew that they would die in God's presence, because of their wickedness (carnalities). Flesh (meaning carnalities) cannot survive in the presence of God, because it is full of sin. Sin is God's enemy. God said no man could look at Him face to face and live. The Israelites knew death was awaiting them if they stared at God face to face. Moses, obviously, had been in God's presence long enough to resemble God's identity. His face was full of God's glory. Therefore the Israelites feared to look at Moses, because he was a mirror image of God's presence (see Exodus 33:11, 20; 34:29–35).

The Dictionary also says to "flourish" means to reach a height of influence. God influences us to be like Him. God grows in us, through us, and on us as we stand in His presence with Him. We should be a mirror image, a reflection of God. God influences us, and we should influence others to be like Him. A righteous man has the benefit of exemplifying the end result of the tree. The end result is a flourishing branch.

Practical Principles
Psalms 51:10

"Created in me a clean heart, O God;
and renew a right spirit within me."

This scripture is vital in our internal growth in God. The vine/branch relationship shows us that through it all, the branch had to be committed to the Vine. For us to be thoroughly committed to God, we have to have a pure sensitive heart. Our heart has to be sensitive to God's voice and His touch. We also have to have a godly spirit flowing within us. If the spirit is that of God, it will help guard our newly created clean God-sensitive heart.

Isaiah 43:7

"Even every one that is called by my name:
for I have created him for my glory, I have
formed him; yea, I have made him."

I, often, attend little league sports activities. I see those little boys and girls performing to the best of their ability. I scan the audience and see the child's parents watching their son or daughter (depending on the sport, and gender performing). Sometimes you don't have to know the parents and their child. You know who has a special relationship based on the parents cheer for their little one. I see the parents smile, and hear their emphatic cheers. It delights me to see the joy the parents are embalmed with. The child is creating glory for their parents. Are you creating glory for He who made you?

Demetrius Smith

Summary Prayer

Glorious God I thank You for the mercy You have given me. I am asking for You to create in me a clean heart and renew in me the right spirit. I desire a heart that is sensitive to Your precious voice, and a spirit that knows when You are trying to lead me. Your divine direction means a lot to me, because You are incapable of failing. Help me to learn how to walk in obedience to the call You have on my life. Give me strength during my weak moments. My desire is to glorify You, and to be Your glorious light that shines in the midst of everyone that might see me. Please heavenly Father, hear my cry, and create the heart inside me what I earnestly desire.

Chapter 8

The Revelation of Holy Things

Who is God? He is one who is worthy of our devotion. He is to be extolled as one of perfection. He says, *"Be ye holy as I am holy" (I Peter 1:16).* God is deeply in love with us. He is so in love with who we are, He declares us to be holy. *"(As it is written in the law of the Lord, Every male that openeth the womb shall be called holy to the Lord;)" (Luke 2:23).* As discussed in the analogy of the vine and branches, God wants us to be symbolic of who He is. God is so passionate about us; He said He would totally wash away our sins (Acts 22:16). He said He would separate us from our sins as far as the east is from the west (Psalms 103:12). God will totally forgive us, so that we can be presented as His holy children.

We are to walk as a transparent to who God is. We know man was created in the image of God Himself—one who was created in God's image; according to God's likeness; one created from God's heart with an incapability of knowing evil, or committing evil before the fall of man. God empowered the creation of His like-imagery to run the earth.

Nothing can limit our actions if no law stands. For instance, if you are driving down a street and you see no stop signs, then you have no law to abide by. Therefore, it permits you to drive without stopping. The appearance of a stop sign in a residential area puts a limit on you while you are driving. If you do not obey the sign that limits you then you have disobeyed the law that put a limit on you.

Was there a law to limit what man could do?

God separated the tree of the knowledge of good and evil for Himself. He told His beloved creation not to eat from this tree. God promised His creation that he would die if he (God's creation) broke the boundary line of eating from this sacred tree. From the moment God made this command, the commandment established a *spiritual law.*

Man, through the devil's schemes, lost focus and failed to heed the command God gave him. Man chose to disobey and eat of the sacred tree that God told him was off limits. In a sense, man was *initially* formed as a 'little god.' He could not backslide or transgress, because he had not; yet, disobeyed God. He totally transcended natural ability.

Man, as a living soul, exceeded natural ability to the extent that nothing God placed in front of him hindered his mental inclination. The first man, Adam, through the breath that God gave him, began giving everything a name:

God: *Here, Adam.*
Adam: *That is fish.*
God: *Look, my son.*
Adam: *That shall be a Camel*
God: *This is for you.*
Adam: *She shall be called woman, because she was taken from man. Her name shall be Eve- (meaning life or mother of all living).*

So we see that Adam was initially created with God-like qualities. What an awesome creation!

God's promise for death was set into motion once Adam ate of the designated tree. The voluntary act to eat from the designated tree is known as the "Adamic fall," or, the fall of man. So there was at least one law that limited man. Adam would have been limitless without a law to limit him, therefore, making him one with God. God is unlimited while man is *limited.* God made a declaration that beside me there is none other (Isaiah 45:5). So He (God) placed a law around man that would limit man from being totally like Him, hence fulfilling the previous described declaration ("beside Me there is none other.")

You say, but Adam was also composed of flesh—His *flesh* also limited him. Flesh did *not* limit Adam. His flesh was incapable of separating him from God provided he did not cross the line. His disobedience activated his flesh (carnalities), and made way for sin to enter life. Adam was similar to Jesus, yet, he was not Jesus. He was similar in the sense that

Jesus was also composed of flesh (this dimension of flesh being that which we see called skin), and knew no sin. Jesus also had a law to abide by. Jesus had to fulfill the plan of God, and die on the cross.

God had to orchestrate a *way* for man to regain authority over sinful flesh (carnalities). The only logical way for God to do this was to overcome sin while walking in flesh (that which we see) as man. God had to walk in an activated flesh and deactivate it by dying *in* it, on the cross.

Remember Jesus is God manifested in the flesh (what we see). Jesus and God are one and the same; therefore, Jesus could not fall as Adam did. If it were not for God manifesting Himself in the flesh (that which we see, being skin), the enemy would have had flesh reigning power. Therefore, God walked in flesh as Jesus. God could not walk in flesh as His persona of the unseen Spirit being, so He used His persona of what could be seen; being Jesus Christ. Jesus in the Hebrew means 'Jehovah saves,' or 'God incarnate.' Christ means "the anointed one." Jesus succeeded—which confirmed God's unlimited capabilities. Jesus also gave man a new opportunity to reign over flesh (meaning our carnalities).

Adam was composed of flesh (skin), and knew no sin until the 'Adamic fall.' God promised Adam if he ate from the tree, he would surely die. Once Adam fell, sin started its reign over man.

Here we see a picture of a man, Adam, obtaining dominion over everything God created. He was incapable of knowing sin, as long as, he heeded

God's instructions. We know Adam did not heed God's instructions, because he ate from the tree!

One of the most selfish things we can do is *blame someone else* for our faults. God began questioning Adam's whereabouts. God asked Adam about the thing he had done. Adam said, "It's the woman's fault,"—the woman God gave to him. She gave him the fruit that he ate. In other words, Adam was saying, "God it is not all my fault. It is hers!"

I told you at the end of Chapter 6, one of the most disturbing feats is for a person to *do wrong* and *act innocent.* God knows all about us. He searches our heart. Man looks on the outer appearance, but God examines the heart (see I Samuel 16:7b). Eve may have felt extremely bad, and maybe worse on account of Adam's blame. She did not know the deep revelation behind the promise from God to Adam. God and Adam might have been the only ones to know the deep revelation. In fact, Adam did not really understand the revelation of the power God granted him. He did not realize the power God invested within him. Let's retrace.

God told Adam that he had been granted dominion over the fish, the birds, every living thing that moves, every herb, every earthly beast, and every tree. God told him to be fruitful and multiply, and replenish the earth. God also granted him, Eve. God placed everything under Adam's authority.

The *only* instruction was for Adam not to eat of the tree of the knowledge of good and evil. The instructions were given directly to Adam. God told

Adam, *"But of the tree of the knowledge of good and evil, thou [you] shalt not eat of it: for in the day that thou [you] eatest thereof thou [you] shalt surely die"* *(Genesis 2:17)*. Isn't it funny how some things are permitted for everyone else, but restricted for you. Isn't it funny how everyone else, seemingly, has no limits, but you? Certain people can go certain places, or do certain things, but you cannot. Your friends can go clubbing, but you have to stay home on Saturday night. Sound familiar?

Next, we see the serpent *beguile* Eve to eat the fruit knowing that she would share it with Adam. The serpent knew the best way to get to Adam was by going through something that meant the most to him. He knew if he went directly to Adam, he (the enemy) would have probably failed. So he used Adam's weakness: Eve, to get to his strength: his obedience to God. Eve was the completion of Adam's life. The enemy used the completing puzzle piece to Adam's fulfillment to cause his (Adam's) separation from God. We know Eve was Adam's weakness, because Adam was *incomplete* until God gave him Eve.

"And Adam gave names to all cattle, and to the fowl of the air, and to every beast of the field; but for Adam there was not found a help meet for him. And the LORD God caused a deep sleep to fall upon Adam, and he slept: and he took one of his ribs, and closed up the flesh instead thereof; and the rib, which the LORD God had taken from man, made he a woman, and brought her to the man. And Adam said, this is now bone of my bones, and flesh of my

flesh: she shall be called Woman, because she was taken out of Man." (Genesis 2:20–23).

Eve ate of the tree, but nothing happened. The Bible says Eve ate and gave some to her husband and he ate. Then immediately following Adam's partaking of the fruit, the Bible says, *"And the eyes of them both were opened" (Genesis 3:7).* Why didn't any thing happen when Eve bit the fruit? Nothing happened because *Adam* was the key to transgressing the law.

God invested such supernatural power in Adam, many people could have eaten of the tree and nothing would have happened (as far as sin and death's reign). God would have probably dealt with them on an individual basis, but their discernment between good and evil would not have appeared. He would have probably dealt with Adam if everyone else touched the fruit except Adam, because he was granted dominion and was responsible for keeping the garden. God laid down a law for Adam to abide by, and he did not prevail. God could have told Adam specifically, "Everyone can eat of the tree except you, and nothing will happen until you eat." God does not give us the total break- down all the time, nor did He give Adam the total breakdown. Sometimes God expects us to simply *trust* and take heed to what He tells us, similar to Abraham and young Isaac.

God told Abraham to offer up Isaac as a sacrifice. He could have told Abraham He (God) had a ram in the bush, but He did not. God wanted to prove Abraham's love and trust. Likewise, God wanted to prove Adam's love and trust for Him. God entrusted Adam with stewardship over His sacred tree.

If many people ate off the tree and Adam followed God's instructions, their eyes would not have opened. Adam was like a *master* light switch among many light switches. We can flip on every switch in the building, and nothing will happen until the master switch is flipped on.

If many people ate from the tree and Adam did not eat from it until he was ninety-nine years old, no one's eyes would have opened until the moment Adam bit into the fruit at ninety-nine years old.

You say, but the Bible says Adam and Eve became one flesh. Therefore, it makes the woman of like-accountability for eating of the fruit. You are right, they did become one. The moment Eve bit of the fruit; the fruit had become lodged in her body, but Adam's participation manifested what Eve had done. Eve's eating of the fruit was nullified, as long as, Adam remained set a part. God said to Adam, *"And unto Adam he said, Because thou hast hearkened unto the voice of thy wife, and hast eaten of the tree, of which I commanded thee, saying, Thou shalt not eat of it: cursed it the ground for thy sake; in sorrow shalt thou eat of it all the days of thy life; (Genesis 3:17)."* Eve was held accountable because:

She was aware of the command not to eat from the tree.

She gained the same revelation from what she ate once Adam ate.

On the contrary, what if Adam would have eaten

and Eve did not eat? Would God have punished Eve for something she did not do? Perhaps God would not have punished her, but she would have suffered, resulting from Adams activity. *"Wherefore, as by one man sin entered into the world, and death by sin; and so death passed upon all men, for all have sinned:" (Romans 5:12).* Therefore, Adam's partaking of the fruit welcomed sin and death into Eve's life. *"Nevertheless death reigned from Adam to Moses, even over them that had not sinned after the similitude of Adams transgression" (Romans 5:14).* Neither you nor I ate from the tree, but we suffer because the master light switch was already flipped on. This was not written to expose Adam's mistake. It was written to reveal unto us that we can cause a tear in the body of Christ if we do not remain conscious and committed to our position in the body of Christ. God has endowed so much power in us. What is the enemy trying to do to get us to transgress against the laws that God has given us?

Let's look at the next revelation. The Bible says, *"and the eyes of them both were opened" (Genesis 3:7).* It is not talking about their *physical* eyes. It is speaking of their *spiritual* eyes. Why would Eve pick and bite the fruit with her eyes closed? How could the serpent point out the tree and refer Eve to look at how good it looked with her eyes *closed* (Genesis 3:1–6)? Why would Eve pass the fruit to Adam and he bite into it with his eyes closed? You know we *have* to see what we are eating! Their physical eyes were already open. When Adam bit the fruit their *spiritual* eyes opened.

As we read the passage, we will notice that the Bible says Adam and Eve knew they were naked after eating the fruit. You may question, "How could they have known they were naked if their physical eyes were not opened?" Once again you are exactly right, but you missed the most important word. The Bible says they "knew" they were naked. They saw the nakedness of each other from the beginning, according to Genesis 2:25, but they had no comprehension of their naked appearance. Before they ate the fruit, the Bible says they were naked and were not ashamed. So they were aware of their nakedness in the beginning. We may think it is impossible to have our eyes open and not be able to see, but this is not so.

There is a notion that during the first stages of a newborn baby's life, the baby's eyes are open, but they really cannot see. They appear to be looking all around, but they have no visual discernment. Or, have you ever seen a person sleeping with their eyes open? They appear to be looking around, aware, but they are asleep, they do not really see. Adam and Eve, initially, lived in similar fashion. They were able to see without spiritual discernment of good versus bad. Their spiritual eyes opened and the gaining of spiritual inclination translated to them, what was previously, an unseen message. Once their spiritual eyes opened they were able to discern the things that only God was able to discern: good and evil.

And the LORD God said, Behold, the man is become as one of us, to know good and evil; and now, lest he put forth his hand, and take also of the tree of life, and eat, and life for ever: Therefore the LORD God sent him forth from the garden of Eden, to till the ground from whence he was taken" (Genesis 3:22–23).

It seemed as though Adam was initially created as a god, (or god-like) because of the way he did things such as name animals without anyone around to tell him what the animal was that he named. In the beginning he only beheld some of God's qualities. Reread the above scripture. We notice that after Adam partook of the fruit is when God declared that man had become as Himself (God). That is why God had to kick him (Adam) out of the garden. Kicking Adam out would keep him from eating from the tree of life. If Adam would have eaten from the tree of life *after* he ate from the tree of knowledge, he would have defiled the Triune supremacy. He would have been like God, even after he sinned by transgressing the law that was laid down for him. He would have been able to live eternally, even with his defiled status.

We know God is incapable of sinning. For Adam to live eternally in a sinful status would have insulted God as Creator. Therefore, God re-established Adam's dwelling place and increased his chores.

A Holy Thing

Throughout the Bible, we see those who understood God's covenant, giving God back a portion of what He had initially given to them. We find people such as Abel, who was the keeper of the sheep, give back to God the firstlings of the fattest portion of his flock. We are able to visit the request from God that every firstborn that opens the womb be set a part for Himself (Exodus13:2). We also discover a womb-barren Hannah praying that God open her womb, and if God were to grant such request she promised to give her firstborn son back to Him (I Samuel 1:11). These are sacred offerings to God.

The tree of the knowledge of good and evil was among God's creations that God set a part for Himself. Among everything God created, this tree was the portion that God conducted as a holy portion of His creations. This tree was considered holy. When Adam touched the tree he defiled a holy thing; something set apart for God. His obedience (not to touch the tree) would have confirmed his appreciation for what God did for him, but he did not obey. He disobeyed, and failed to understand the outcome of his disobedience.

If Hannah had not discovered the importance of God's request toward the firstborn child, she may have never had a child. The Lord gave the instructions to set apart the firstborn child during the deliverance of Israel's bondage to Egypt. God told Moses to give the instructions to Israel. With these instructions, Moses also told the people to remember the day they came out of bondage through the parting of the Red Sea. Obviously, Hannah was aware of what God told Moses. God granted Hannah's request for a child. God parted her womb so a child could pass through the bondage of her "barrenness."

One of the main laws requiring our obedience is in regards to our tithes and offerings (Malachi 3:9). This too, is a symbol of the sacredness of the holy tree. God has separated tithes and offerings among everything else He has given us. He has designated them as holy unto Him. He instructed us not to touch them, or else we open the door for curses to enter into our life (Malachi 3:8). God says we ask, "How can we rob You, God?" Then He gives the answer—we rob Him by *keeping* the designated holy portion of our substance. We are eating the fruit of a holy tree when we refrain from paying our tithes and offerings. God asked us not to touch the tree. We must separate the portion due Him, as a voluntary act of reverence, and worship to God. He has no problem blessing His saints. He does have a problem in granting our request when we fail to fulfill His requirements.

He promised that we will be cursed if we fail to keep the holy tree sacred. The results of Adam not taking heed to God's instructions were not pleasant. God told Eve her disobedience provided great sorrow and conception; and she would birth children in travail (pain). He also placed the wife in submission to her husband. Adam would be forced to farm a "cursed" ground, and now toil for things that were originally freely given. God also told Adam the day he ate from the tree he (Adam) would die (Genesis 2:17). It seemed like Adam was still living after he ate the fruit. Adam only appeared to be living. The moment he ate the fruit, the hourglass was flipped into motion. At the immediate point Adam took of the tree, in came sin and his living timeline.

Adam was living in eternity before the Adamic fall. An introduction to sin and death crept into his life after the Adamic fall (Romans 5:12). This is also the moment flesh (carnalities) became an enemy to the Spirit. God promised us that curses would fall upon us if we fail to heed His instructions. The reality is that even if we do not take heed, God will get His tithe and offerings one way or another. If we get sick and have to go to the doctor, those doctors may be the one paying tithes with our money. Some people do not pay tithes and offerings, and they wonder why their appliances constantly need repairing. God will get His tithes through the repairmen, and certain people suffer for their disobedience. Some of us may not have to call plumbers, or take our children to the doctor if we would pay our tithes. We can give our tithe to God, and keep our health. It is absurd for us to be the one that suffers, and God still get what He requested.

If we follow the instructions to pay our tithe, God promises to respond by opening His windows of heaven on our life. He says He will rebuke the devourer for our sakes (Malachai 3:11), and allow our harvest to come at the appointed time. When the fruit comes forth at its appointed time it is ripe. Fruit that comes too early is not ripe, and sometimes mushy. If fruit is too late the chances of production is minimal. So our preference is for our blessings to come at their appointed time. Provided we obey God's instructions, these are some of the blessings He promises us. It takes deep faith to keep holy things holy.

Unconditional Love

God's love is unconditional. Even in Adam's disobedience, God took action on the one who persuaded Adam's action. Anything God creates, He does it in *His* likeness with divine purpose. Everything during the first six days of creation, the Bible completes the day by saying God saw what He created was *good.* Just to be *like* God is awesome.

God took action against the serpent when the serpent disturbed what He created. The serpent planted contagious seeds in the mind of Eve. Adam picked up on what the serpent told Eve, and allowed those seeds to lead him (Adam) astray. Adam was holy; he was anointed. No normal human being would be able to look at a four-footed, snout-nosed beast and name it 'pig.' Then turn around to hear a beautiful lullaby being chirped by a winged plane and call it, 'bird.' Adam was amazingly anointed.

To be holy is to be set apart, sacred for God's use. This is who Adam was. God placed him in the garden and told him to dress it. That is like having a well dressed mansion, decked with some Le Corbusier furniture, a pearl off-white staircase, surrounding a crystal clear angel fountain, a plasma television that falls from the ceiling, and you telling your child that the house is his. You just want him to keep it clean and updated. The child has to be trained to maintain a home with such features. He must also be clear-minded, not given to foolishness.

Adam was created of such maturity. He beheld God's qualities, which permitted him trust from God. God knew exactly who He had created. God's love for Adam was so pure God cursed the enemy for touching His anointed creation. Adam touched a holy thing, and brought curses on his life. The serpent touched a holy thing with his mouth, and brought curses on his life. It is critical for you to understand what God has set aside as a holy thing. God loved Adam enough to take a stance against the serpent. Although He removed Adam from the garden, He loved him enough not to kill him the very second Adam took a taste of death.

During King David's reign, a servant named Uzzah died for putting his hands on the "Ark of the Covenant." The Ark of the Covenant was a symbol of the Holy of Holies; which is the place where God dwelt in the Old Testament. God, as a place for His dwelling presence, designated the Ark during Old Testament biblical days. Uzzah was trying to do what he felt was right. He saw the Holy Ark about to fall over and tried to cease its fall (2 Samuel 6:6, 7). He died when he touched the Ark, because carnal things cannot handle spiritual things. He was not designated to handle something as holy as the Ark. He was trying to handle the Ark in a defiled status. God Forbid!

Our tithes and offering are considered holy things. The Virgin Mary was considered holy enough to birth a holy child. As a matter of fact, an angel told Mary, *"The Holy Ghost shall come upon thee, and the power of the Highest shall overshadow thee: therefore also that holy thing which shall be born of thee shall be call the Son of God" (Luke 1:35).* The angel declared Jesus to be a holy thing. Joseph understood the value of his wife. Therefore, he bid not to make Mary a public example. Back in early biblical history, it was customary to stone a woman who committed adultery. This is the example Mary had portrayed. She was not pregnant by having relations with her husband.

How can a woman become impregnated, and say she does not know how she became pregnant? The normal response would be, because she had sex with someone!

Joseph must have had some type of relationship with God to buy into the belief of a Holy Ghost impregnation. Mary impregnated by the Holy Ghost?

Joseph must have known God. He reverenced God and respected his wife enough to keep this situation behind closed doors. Not only did he keep it quite, but the Bible also says he did not have sex with Mary until after her firstborn son was birthed.

We, previously, learned of the law God gave to Moses regarding every firstborn child. Jesus was Mary's firstborn child. Wow! God set this plan in motion years before, to cover the charges of Mary's firstborn son who would be named Jesus! Joseph did not touch his holy wife with his hands, or his mouth. Nor did he touch the holy child inside her by cross-pollinating his corrupt seed with the pure seed within Mary through having relations with her, thus, defiling the purity of her Holy Spirit impregnation.

Mary and Joseph gave their son back to God. In turn, they received the biggest blessing they could have ever asked for. Not only did they receive a huge blessing, so did we! God loved Mary enough to use her to birth a gift to the world. Joseph loved God and his wife enough to keep the family together.

God considers us to be holy. He asks that we be holy as He is holy. That means He wants us to present our body a living sacrifice, holy, and acceptable to Him (Romans 12:1). He demands that we respect, and set boundary lines around ourselves. He considers us like He considered Jesus.

For as many as are led by the Spirit of God, they are the sons of God. For ye have not received the spirit of bondage again to fear; but ye have received the Spirit of Adoption, whereby we cry, Abba, Father. The Spirit itself beareth witness with our spirit, that we are the children of God: And if children, then heirs; heirs of God, and joint-heirs with Christ; if so be that we suffer with him, that we may be also glorified together" (Roman 8:13–17).

You mean to tell me beyond all the mistakes we have made; God is giving us the opportunity to be a joint-heir with Jesus Christ? Jesus Christ was powerful! Am I telling you we can obtain the same

promises and power as Jesus? Yes! That is exactly
what I am saying. We must see ourselves as God sees
us; He says we are the *"apple of his eye" (Psalms
17:8) (Zechariah 2:8)!* He views us as sons and
daughters, and not bastard children with no father.
For those who do not know their father in the physical, our supernatural Father has always been there
for us. He wants to engraft us back into our rightful
position. His holy apostle said *"But my God shall
supply all your need according to his riches in glory
by Christ Jesus" (Philippians 4:19).* God loves us
just that much!

Faith in What He Says

There is almost nothing that can separate a
person who heavily believes in something, from that
belief. Once a person has their mind set a certain way,
it is nearly impossible to alter their thinking. Adam
lost belief in what God promised. If he had believed
death would definitely appear once he ate of the
tree, perhaps he would not have chanced his destiny.
His faith in God diminished. The enemy told Adam
something that caused Adam to doubt the severity of
God's promise. The very second God tells us something; it immediately becomes a law or a promise.

God told Israel to sanctify every firstborn child.
Immediately a law was established. He told Adam
not to eat of the tree. From that point a law was laid
down. Then He told Adam the day he ate of the tree
he would surely die. At that point God established
a promise. God tells us to give tithes and offerings.

He immediately laid down a law for us. If we do not obey (by withholding our tithes and offerings), God says we are cursed with a curse. Here is where God establishes a promise.

We have to believe what God has said shall come to pass. Whatever He has told us will not slack. He asked us to pay our tithes and offerings for *our* benefit. When we pay them, it acknowledges the trust we have in God. It silently shows our reverence for God, and obedience to His Word. The act of paying tithes and offerings helps us remain actively involved in our belief in God. It takes deep faith to pay tithes when we have one hundred dollars to our name, a hundred and thirty dollar bill due, and a ten percent tithe law. Calculate it!

What would you do?

Do you pay the tithe and trust God to provide? Or, do you put all the money toward your due bill, still do not get it paid on time, and go home to find out you have to pay to get one of the house appliances fixed for not paying your tithe? It also takes deep faith for a millionaire to be a millionaire, and know he has at least a $100,000 tithing commandment hanging over his head. Try to put yourself in that position. Would you pay your tithe? Or, would you take the risk of not paying them and putting someone in your household in danger of sickness or disease, because of the curse that "you" allow to enter your life.

Much like Adam, whenever we reject to follow any of the laws God has given us, "we" give the enemy an entrance way into our lives. The enemy is who God says He will rebuke when we pay our tithes, but God calls the enemy, "the devour." By no means am I saying that if we follow all of the guidelines, that we won't have any sickness, death, or other worries. I am saying that if we abide by the guidelines that God has promised us that He will work on our behalf. God never brings evil on His people, He does allow certain things to happen to us to prove us and build us like He did Job. It is one thing for God to allow it, and another thing for "us" to freely open the door to the enemy. We welcome the enemy into our lives when we reject God's commandments. No matter what the situation is, the failure of not paying our tithes is unaffordable. When we honor God with our giving, He promises us over-flowing blessings (Malachi 3:10).

We have to believe that God's promises are true. We have to believe if we keep the holy tree sacred, God will watch over our situation. It shows how much we care about God, as opposed to, focusing solely on our problems. God knows all about our struggles. The question is do we believe He would ask us to pay our tithes and offerings without considering our struggles? Do we really believe God is that inconsiderate?

Money is one of the most important things to man and is precisely why God chose the tithe as a test for obedience. This is why He says we cannot serve two masters. *"No man can serve two masters: for either he will hate the one, and love the other; or else he will hold to the one, and despise the other. Ye can-*

not serve God and mammon" (Matthew 6:24). Either money will draw our love, or God will draw our love. The most awesome thing is God can double; triple, or even quadruple what we give Him. What is more amazing, is God will give what He rolls over, back to us. This is God's give/receive law.

He will also reward our trust in Him by paying our tithes, and bless us in other ways. It might not be money that you need. God knows this too. He will reconciliate a broken marriage, save a wayward child, give us a peaceful mind, or repair our wounded spirit. God knows what we have need of. We have to believe that what God sets aside as holy shall remain holy. God gave us authority over a portion of the holy tree. It is our job to keep our portion holy. This also applies to our body. We have to keep ourselves holy. We are a holy child of God. So believe it, and act accordingly.

Practical Principles

John 15:13

"Greater love hath no man than this, that a man lay down his life for his friends."

Would you sacrifice your child's life for a multitude of backstabbers, whoremongers, and thieves? That is what our God did for us. He unselfishly gave away His only true companion for you and me. We owe Him our life. God's love for us is so unconditional that He suffered extreme pain by giving His only Son in exchange for us. I don't believe you would give up your endearing children for another stranger, or would you?

I Peter 1:15

"But as he which hath called you is holy, so be ye holy in all manner of conversation."

The word 'conversation' in its use here means 'lifestyle.' If we understood all of the benefits that come with living holy, we would do whatever it took not to sacrifice a holy lifestyle. I know it is a battle to go against the natural grains of life. Christianity is not some patty-cake walk, but what in life is? We make a big deal about being a Christian for many reasons. Some reasons are we don't want to change, we are afraid we will lose some things, we don't feel like we are worthy of God, and we cannot see the benefits.

Why is it when our parents tell us not to do something we do it anyway? It is often because we think they are trying to keep us from something? Later we find out their direction was for our good. Being holy inherits the same benefit. It is for our own good. Yeah, we will make mistakes, but all God asks is for us to ask for forgiveness with a pure heart.

Summary Prayer

Father, I thank you from the depths of my heart for sharing your beloved Son with me. I know You did not have to choose me, but I am glad You did. I don't know how You could save someone like me, neither do I challenge Your sovereign power. Thank You God. I really thank You. I praise You for who You are to me. You are holy; therefore, I shall be holy.

Help me work on fulfilling Your holy call on my life. I understand it is a benefit for being Your child. Help me see the benefits. One benefit is my life, and I thank You graciously. In Jesus name I pray, Amen!

Chapter 9

A Living Dead Man

Everything that Jesus performed, said, and did, God gave Him the ability to do. You know why? Jesus was a man who knew God's heart. He possessed the heart of God. He was deeply concerned about becoming the man God ordained Him to become. Jesus understood who He was; therefore, He walked according to the fulfillment of His destiny. He did not compromise His walk—His walk became His lifestyle. His lifestyle was comprised of fellowship, prayer, worship, praise, and honoring God. All of these spiritual weapons were under-girded by His faith in God. Jesus was a man of humility and submission. He was full of love and compassion.

Jesus knew God's heart because He was God walking in the flesh. The Bible says *"He grew strong in spirit, was filled with wisdom, and the grace of God was upon him" (Luke 2:40).* We can walk like Jesus did.

How can we grow strong in spirit? We grow

strong in spirit by use of the same spiritual interactions Jesus exemplified.

What about gaining wisdom? *"If any of you lack wisdom, let him ask of God, that giveth to all (men) liberally, and upbraideth not (to find no fault once he gives it to you); and it shall be given him"* (James 1:5).

How can a person obtain grace? Grace is God's unmerited favor. He gives grace to whom He chooses. No one is worthy of it. The love of Jesus makes us worthy to receive it.

Jesus spent time with teachers listening and asking questions (Luke 2:46). He knew what was traditional, and He knew the laws. More importantly, Jesus knew who His *enemy* was. Some of us cannot function correctly because we have no idea who our enemy is. Some of us think that our enemy is the man next door, or that relative in our home. By far, are we mistaking them to be our real enemy? The enemy may be using them to come against us, but they are not our enemy. Jesus had a deep understanding of this. He knew who His enemy was.

Jesus' relationship with God was so pure and deep, He saw things like God saw them. God was able to use Jesus' life to bring glory to Himself, because Jesus was willing to be used. Jesus laid down His life for God while living on earth before the cross, and he laid it down again on the cross. *Jesus was a living dead man.* He *died to the man,* but *lived through the Spirit.* Being that His relationship with God was so compassionate, He was able to see things like God saw them in every aspect of His life—just like the time He decided to travel by boat, across the Sea of Galilee, to a country on the opposite side of Capernaum. (Capernaum is a village located alongside the sea where Jesus taught and performed miracles). Jesus was placed in a position where His spiritual discernment was critically imperative.

On the opposite side of Capernaum, in the country of Gadarenes, lived an insane man. The Bible says this man "dwelled among the tombs." It was common for him to be in the mountains crying aloud and cutting himself with stones. He was so defiant, no one could lock him down with chains. The authorities tried that tactic before only to witness his human strength. The obnoxious man pulled the chain from out of the ground, and broke the chain into pieces. No one could tame the man, discipline him, or calm him. He had an unclean spirit inside him.

Could Jesus have known there was a demon-possessed man in this country?

The Spirit within Jesus knows all men, *"But Jesus did not commit himself unto them, because he knew all men, And needed not that any should testify of man: for he knew what was in man" (John 2:23,24).* Jesus was God walking in the flesh. Nevertheless, news travels fast by word of mouth. The people of Gadarenes must have feared a man of such insanity. I can imagine everyone within the vicinity spreading the word across the region that there was a madman in Gadarenes. People tend to refrain from being in the presence of a person this violent. Everyone within the area probably looked at the man with contempt.

You remember how your parents told you, "Don't you go around there messing with that boy/girl, you know they are crazy!" I can imagine the people in Gadarenes talking like that. I can hear one person tell another how crazy and evil this man was. I see them depicting him as one of their enemies. I also envision the elders telling the younger to stay away from this man's area, because he was a cold-hearted madman.

Then enters the country of the Gadarenes a man named Jesus. Jesus and His disciples arrived safe and sound, out of a ravaging storm, to the country of Gadarenes. When Jesus stepped out of the ship and onto the shore, this demon-possessed man welcomed him. The Bible says when the man saw Jesus he ran and worshipped him.

Can you imagine seeing a madman who no one can tame or discipline have a 'Jesus sighting,' and watch him run to submit himself to Jesus' authority? I am talking about a man with the strength to break a chain into pieces, bully anyone who steps foot on what he declared was his territory, had the ignorance to cut himself with whatever he could find, slept in the graveyards, refrained from hearing anyone because of his rebellion, then that same man has a 'Jesus sighting' and immediately bows down in His presence. He recognized the Lord. Whoa!

It is evident Jesus did not look at the man as His enemy, because Jesus focused on the unclean spirit controlling the man when the man started to speak. Jesus commanded the spirit to come out of the man. Then He asked the man what His name was, and the man replied, "Legion: which means many." The Bible says He was demon possessed. He had many demonizing spirits controlling Him, (see Mark 5:1–19).

Jesus had such a well-defined relationship with God that He was able to see the man through the eyes of God. He knew this man was not the enemy. The enemy was *using* the man's body as his habitation. What is so profound about this story is the fact that Jesus did not have to say a word. *All Jesus had to do was show up!*

Don't you think it would be nice to just show up on the scene and watch demons tremble? The continuity of Jesus relationship with God demanded such power; likewise, our relationship with God through Jesus.

The lifestyle Jesus lived on earth teaches us a valuable lesson in how to overcome, and be as potent as He was on earth. God manifested Himself in the flesh to show us how to overcome life encounters. He also came to take back what the enemy stole from Him: the purity of His people.

Jesus sailed over to Gadara to free a man who was being manipulated by the adversary. Jesus cared enough for the man not to allow the enemy to continue to torment him (the man). Once the man was delivered, Jesus told him to go tell the good news to everyone. This would consist of the man's belief in the power of Jesus. Once he confessed Jesus he would gain an opportunity to receive salvation.

Jesus went to the country of the Gadarenes to take a soul back that the enemy tried to steal. This action, in return, would bring glory to God. In part, it also shows us how to take back what the enemy has stolen from us. Jesus walked this earth with a dependency on God that only a crack addict on crack could relate to—not to demean the addict, because we all have our problems. Jesus is potent enough to deliver us all. Jesus loosed His desires for oneness with God. He was delighted in God to the point that *God's* desires became *His* desires. God, therefore, was able to give Jesus the desires of His heart. *"Delight thyself also in the LORD; and he shall give thee the desires of thine heart" (Psalm 37:4).* Jesus' desires were actually the desires of God's heart for His life, and not His own; this due in part to the deep communion Jesus has with God.

It is sort of like falling in love with a newfound friend. When we fall in love with someone we tend to forget about ourselves, and we put their interest in place of our own. The reason we put our interest aside for their interest, is because we have decided to lay down *our* life for a friend. As a result, their desires passionately become our desires. We begin to do what they want. If it is true love it is not a control issue, it is a love affair. This is the type of relationship Jesus and God have. Jesus was a *living dead man* while living on earth.

A Walking Miracle

The enemy is very schematic in everything he does. Just as God has a purpose for our lives, so does the devil. We walk through life making choices that will determine our final destination. Our final destination will either be heaven or hell. We will either live in eternal peace, or we will be forever separated from God in a fiery hell. If accidentally touching a hot rack in a hot oven can detach my skin, hell is not a place I want to be.

The devil knows how real judgment day is, so he tries to keep us blinded from the truth. He does whatever it takes to get us to rebel against God. He wants us to be rebellious against what God tells us to do or not to do. He subtly tries to lead us into rebellion.

The enemy will tell us it is okay not to pay our tithes this week, because that money should be used for something more important. He will tell us that we can make up this weeks tithe amount on a later date. If God tells us to sow a seed toward ministry, the enemy will sow a negative seed into our mind and tell us that God did not really tell us to sow that seed. The enemy will tell us the preacher is trying to use our money for himself, or that they do not really need our money. The adversary cautiously leads us into rebellion. *"For rebellion is as the sin of witchcraft"* *(I Samuel 15:23a).*

Witchcraft is a part of the manifested works of the flesh. *"Now the works of the flesh are manifest, which are these . . .idolatry,* **witchcraft**, *hatred*

. . .I have also told you in time past, that they which do such things shall not inherit the kingdom of God" (Galatians 5:18–21). Earlier in chapter eight we talked a little about flesh being God's enemy. *"Because the carnal mind is enmity against God: for it is not subject to the law of God, neither indeed can be. So then they that are in the flesh cannot please God" (Romans 8:6, 7).*

God likens rebellion to witchcraft. When we rebel against God we are performing witchcraft. Witchcraft is a manifested work of the flesh (carnalities). Carnality is God's enemy. When the enemy leads us to rebel against God, we are acting as his (the devil's) companion; therefore, we become an enemy to God. If this is not already enough, God said we would not inherit the Kingdom of God by 'fiddling' with such nastiness.

One of the inheritances gained in the Kingdom of God is the ability to walk similar to Jesus. *"The Spirit itself beareth witness with our spirit (the spirit of God that dwells within us), that we are the children of God. And if children, then heirs; heirs of God, and joint-heirs with Christ" (Romans 8:17).* To be able to do the things Jesus did is an inheritance, like speaking to confused situations and commanding them to line up. Our inheritance is taken away from us when we walk under the influence of the enemy.

It is safe to say that "Legion" was acting as God's enemy, because he was extremely rebellious. Jesus could have acted as everyone else did toward Legion, but he did not. Some of the people tried to bind the man with chains. They tried to bind a demon in the flesh. They lacked the spiritual discernment required to calm the man. Jesus knew the enemy had possessed the man. Legion established an area that made everyone believe he owned it, except Jesus. *When Jesus shows up things must change!!!* Jesus does not tolerate anyone believing that the enemy has reigning power, nor does he tolerate the enemy's foolishness in persuading people to believe that he (the enemy) reigns.

Jesus showed up to cast the demons out of the man. Again, Jesus had the spiritual discernment to see that this man was not the enemy. He stepped onto the scene. The demons acknowledged who Jesus was, asked Jesus for permission to leave the man, and enter some swine nearby. Then Jesus rebuked the demons, casting them out, freeing the man. That is so awesome!

The demons inside the man asked Jesus could they leave a place they really wanted to stay. Why? They feared Jesus. *"Thou believest that there is one God; thou doest well: the devils also believe, and tremble" (James 2:19).* My God! Not only that, Jesus showed that the enemy does not have ownership over anything he pretends to have. The enemy did not own the man, or the land.

The Scripture said we are heirs of God, and joint-heirs with Jesus Christ. God has given *us* the opportunity to walk and perform miracles like Jesus did. We also have the same inheritance as Jesus does. The devil knows this, so he tries to keep us in a cloud of darkness. He subtly approaches us with things that make perfect sense, but they are contrary to God's instructions. It makes sense to put our tithes on the back burner to pay a due bill, and pay the tithes back when we can. The thing is that those things lead us into being rebellious to what God instructed us to do. The enemy has this understanding. If we are not walking *with* God, we are walking *against* God. The enemy wants us to walk contrary to God, so that we will be walking alongside *him* (the enemy).

We might not curse, steal, or kill. Just because we do not, does not mean we are not rebelling against God. Rebellion denotes *any* performance that goes against the flow of what God told us to do, or not to do. Our rebellion to what God has instructed us to do buys us a spot with the enemy.

Once we understand the schemes of the enemy we will be able to expose him (the enemy) for what he is: a liar! *"When he speaketh a lie, he speaketh of his own: for he is a liar, and the father of it" (John 8:44).* When we expose him, we have the opportunity to resist him. Once we openly resist him, he must go. *"Submit yourselves therefore to God. Resist the devil, and he will flee from you" (James 4:7).* We have reigning power over the enemy through Jesus. This is a part of the inheritance.

The first thing we must learn how to do is interact with God. We have to develop a compassionate relationship with God. In the process of developing a compassionate relationship with God, we will begin to replace our desires with His desires for our life. We will start dying to our own ways in the midst of this process. We start dying to the things that are natural for us to do. We begin to die to those natural things we *do* like: cursing, lying, stealing, being deceptive just to name a few. Those bad old habits will start flaking off our lives like rust.

We are actually dying to ourselves when we die to our old ways and habits. We must crucify our flesh for the benefit of the Kingdom. We have to endure the wounds that others inflict upon us for the Kingdom. These explanations define what Jesus meant when He told us to "take up our cross and follow him." We have to endure our hardships, almost, daily.

Apostle Paul said, *"As it is written, For thy sake we are killed all the day long; we are accounted as sheep for the slaughter" (Roman 8:36).* When our relationship with God becomes as passionate as Jesus' was, we start living a daily lifestyle of sacrificing ourselves for God. *"I beseech you therefore, brethren, by the mercies of God, that ye present your bodies a living sacrifice, holy, acceptable unto God, [which is] your reasonable service" (Romans 12:1).* Paul profoundly defined it when he said present our bodies "a living sacrifice."

When we die to ourselves we are being crucified for the sake of the spiritual realm. It feels like the pressures of life are killing us, but they are inaugurated to help us grow spiritually. The quicker we decide to die to ourselves, the earlier God will be able to resurrect us from the grave. The grave is our metamorphic tool for spiritual death to self. On our third day in the grave God will glorify us as His walking miracle!

Metamorphosis

One of the most common stories we hear about when someone talks about metamorphism pertains to the butterfly. We love to apply the end result of a worm changing to a beautiful butterfly to our daily life building process. The butterfly is a good simile to use when describing what the end result of our life should resemble. The life of the butterfly reminds me of my stay with my grandparents.

My grandparents have about five or six trees that are shaped like Christmas trees. They are all about ten feet tall. These trees are lined up like a fence alongside the north side of their house. When I was young, I noticed that from these trees would grow little cocoons. I had one friend that would come over everyday he saw me outside, and we would pick these cocoons off the tree. We would pull the cocoons off the tree, and then peel them open like a banana. Whenever we peeled the cocoons open, I noticed that there was life inside the cocoon. This life was that of a worm, or caterpillar. We were nasty enough to pull those little worms out of their cocoon (no limits to a boy's curiosity). We would examine them, drop the worm and the cocoon on the ground, and then pull another cocoon from the tree. We would do this for a little while before we moved to our next adventure. We did not do this every single day, but we would dissect those cocoons whenever it crossed our mind.

Very ignorant to why or what those cocoons were for, they were there for a reason. The only thing we knew, in our young minds, was that my grandparents had a "worm tree." We mistakenly felt like those little worms were dying inside those cocoons. We thought the worms were waiting for someone to come and free them from those sealed cocoons. Worms were supposed to crawl on the ground, and not hang from a tree. The sight of those incarcerated worms made us think they were held captive by their predator. Even though it was fun to peel the cocoon, we held sentiments for the worm's feelings. Far as we knew, we were doing them a favor by delivering them from the cocoon.

As I began to maturate in life, I realized that there is validity in the accommodations of those cocoons. Those cocoons were really there for a purpose. The purpose that was set was not for negative reasoning. It was not like a predator shot the cocoon around the worm to secure the worm as its prey. The worm emits a substance, a lining around itself to formulate the cocoon. The worm uses the cocoon to hibernate inside of it, for the development of the end result—making preparation to become a butterfly.

The worm naturally knows the cocoon's purpose as part of the process—if the worm does not go through the hibernating stage inside the cocoon, it will not reach its destiny. The worm must go through the pain of isolation. It must endure lonely days and nights of being in a tight spot. The tight structure of the cocoon helps to secure the body as it goes through metamorphosis, from a worm to a butterfly. Once the wings develop in strength, the new creature forcefully detaches itself from inside the cocoon.

My friend and I were actually hurting those worms. We altered their destiny when we extracted them from their cocoons. We crippled the promise of many worms. We believed we were doing the worms a favor, but we were changing the course of their lives. They believed that they would one day float in beauty on the surface of the air, only to find themselves lying dormant on the ground. It was our assistance to those worms that stagnated their promise. We obstructed the metamorphosis it takes for the worm to transform into a butterfly.

This is what the enemy desires to do to us. He wants to stagnate our spiritual growth. He will obstruct the path of our spiritual growth however he can. The enemy desires to sift us as wheat (see Luke 22:39). He wants to break us until we crumble into pieces.

If we fall, we have to get back up. *"For a just [man] falleth seven times, and riseth up again" (Proverbs 24:16a).* If we make a mistake, like fornication for example, we need to repent and ask God for forgiveness. I have made many mistakes during my spiritual growth. I, graciously, thank God for looking upon my heart. I thank Him for forgiving me, and affording me the opportunity to witness to you in this book.

As we can see, God has shown us some of His secret revelations. He forgave me for my failures, and He still continues to share His everlasting love with me. We cannot allow the enemy to use our shortcomings to separate us from God. *If God says He forgives us, no devil in hell can change the outcome.* We need to have faith that God will forgive us. *"To give knowledge of salvation unto his people by the remission (forgiveness) of their sins" (Luke 1:77).* The only time God will not forgive us is when we try to take advantage of the grace He affords us, or if we speak against the Holy Ghost. *"For if we sin willfully after that we have received the knowledge of the truth, there remaineth no more sacrifice for sins" (Hebrews 10:26 and Mark 3:29).* Expose the enemy for what he is worth, the profit of a liar—which is damnation!

Expose

The enemy knows more about some of us than we know about ourselves. He has watched the process of people's lives enough to know what the end result should be. He has observed slimy worms turn into butterflies over and over again. He knows what we are supposed to become, and he despises us and our potential destiny. He has pulled many people from the "worm tree" before they reached their final development. The only difference is he does not have the upper hand as, my friend and I, had over the worms on that "worm tree."

We have the ability to fight back and overcome what the enemy desires to do. He has peeled open the cocoon and exposed us to some things that are detrimental to our destiny. We can either fight back while going through metamorphosis, or we can give in to what he offers us. The end result of his offer will drop us, and the cocoon on the ground. Then he will pick another cocoon off the worm tree to dissect the life inside of it.

If I were totally ignorant, I would have believed every worm we found inside the cocoon was dead. I bet, sometimes, the worm wishes it could press its way into developing wings faster. It has no place to go but to have faith that nature will take its course. The worm or caterpillar is in a position where the only thing it can do is believe its time is coming; just on the horizon. It believes that one day, soon to come, it will have the strength in its newly formed wings to crack open the cocoon. Once those wings develop, the worm realizes that time has transformed into its promise. The price has been paid to gain the benefit of transitioning from a impoverished crawl on pavement, to a rich flight in the air.

The wings are not the only thing gained as payment for enduring the process. There is also the benefit of having glorious colors painted on its wings. The re-created being also goes from being called a worm to being called a fly, but no ordinary fly—it is called a butterfly.

When we see a worm we, simply, say look at that worm. If we could see the spiritual promise and potential of certain worms while they are crawling on the ground, we would say, "Look at that butterfly!" We lack the spiritual discernment necessary to see the worm's outcome. We look past the metamorphosis the worm will go through to fulfill its destiny. Once it lives through the process, the process will transform it into one of life's most beautiful creations.

We have witnessed the act of a worm become a butterfly so many times that we know what certain worms are made to become. The enemy has been just as observant of God's people. He knows God's people have promises. The enemy knows we have massive potential. This is the process he wants to stop. He does not want us to fulfill our beautiful outcome. If we transform into anything, he wants us to transform into one of his (the devil's) worthless associates.

"Ye do the deeds of your father. Then said they to him (Jesus), We be not born of fornication; we have one Father, [even] God. Jesus said unto them, If God were your Father, ye would love me: for I proceeded forth and came from God; neither came I of myself, but he sent me. Why do ye not understand my speech? [even] because ye cannot hear my word. Ye are of [your] father the devil, and the lusts of your father ye will do. He was a murderer from the beginning, and abode not in the truth, because there is no truth in him. When he speaketh a lie, he speaketh of his own: for he is a liar, and the father of it. And because I tell [you] the truth, ye believe me not. Which of you convinceth me of sin? And if I say the truth, why do ye not believe me? He that is of God heareth God's words: ye therefore hear [them] not, because ye are not of God" (John 8:41–47).

This is what the devil wants to do. He wants

to fool us. He wants us to abort our destiny. If we are already with God, he wants us to transition from righteousness to damnation. If we are searching for God, the enemy wants to detach our wondering mind from grabbing hold of God.

God views us as a butterfly while we are still crawling on the ground. He calls us a butterfly when we look like a nasty worm. *"But we are all as an unclean [thing], and all our righteousnesses [are] as filthy rags; and we all do fade as a leaf; and our iniquities, like the wind, have taken us away" (Isaiah 64:6).* Aside from us being filthy, God declared that we be set aside for Him right after birth. Remember I told you earlier that God laid a law that every child that opens the womb be declared holy. *"(As it is written in the law of the Lord, Every male that openeth the womb shall be called holy to the Lord;)" (Luke 2:23).* While we are walking in filthiness, God looks upon us as holy.

God has the spiritual discernment to see our destiny. Just like God gave Abram a sign of his destiny by calling him, Abraham, He gives us a sign of *our* destiny. He gives us a sign by calling us names like: *chosen* (I Peter 2:9), *God's elect* (Colossians 3:12), super *conqueror* (Romans 8:37), *precious* (Isaiah 43:4), *joint-heir* (Romans 8:17), *Blessed* (Psalms 32), and the *apple of His eye* (Psalm 17:8) to name a few.

God calls us names that associate us with the destiny He has purposed for us. The apple has to start off as a seed in the ground before the seed manifests apples. God calls us the apple of His eye as a symbol of our destiny. He calls us by the precious potential He has invested inside us. He calls us certain names while we are working on becoming that which He called us to be. God expects us to die to ourselves and endure metamorphosis, in order, to become a butterfly.

One of the outcomes of metamorphosis is being able to see things like Jesus did. Jesus had a wealth full of spiritual discernment. Jesus went through the stages of life necessary to be as potent as He was on earth. This is why Jesus was so powerful. He had clueless faith in God. He was obedient to what God wanted. *"Behold, to obey is better than sacrifice (I Samuel 15:22b)."* God cannot use us if we opt out of hearing His directions for our life.

If Jesus were caught up in being well known, or in pleasing people, He would not have performed some of His miracles. Under the old mosaic laws (laws Moses gave the children of Israel) it was unlawful to do any work, even the working of miracles, on the Sabbath day. The Sabbath is a day of holiness and rest.

Jesus went into the synagogue one Sabbath day. The synagogue was a place where Jesus often taught. When He entered the synagogue, there was a man inside that had a withered hand. Everyone within the synagogue watched Jesus to see what His reaction would be in respects to this man. *"And they watched him, whether he would heal him on the Sabbath day; that they might accuse him" (Mark 3:2).* If Jesus had not been obedient to God, He would have looked over the man's ailment. Jesus told the man to get up. Then He asked the Pharisees (religious people; those that new God's word, but lacked a relationship with God), *"Is it lawful to do good on the Sabbath days, or to do evil? To save life, or to kill?" (Mark 2:4).* No one had an answer to His questions, because they were stuck in their ways.

The man stuck out his withered hand, and it was made whole like his other one. The Pharisees then went to confer with the Herodians, which were a religious political group, to destroy Jesus for what He had done on the Sabbath. Jesus was looking to be obedient to God by doing His (God) will.

Jesus was not into making friends or pleasing anyone when it came to His relationship with God. His love for God caused Him to lose many "so-called" friends. He lost their respect, and many became His enemies. Even in that respect the Proverb declares, *"When a man's ways please the LORD, he (God) maketh even his (your) enemies to be at peace with him (you)" (Proverbs 16:7).*

I can remember a few times when I saw people I knew hated me. For some reason they started to bop their head (as in saying, "Hi,") when they saw me. I knew they did not mean it. I could not understand what promoted the drastic change after many years of watching them cut, and roll their eyes at me. Now that I know Proverbs 16:7, I finally understand why. God said He would make our enemies be at peace with us.

When we gain continuity with God, *our* enemies

become *His* enemies. God did say He would *"curse him that curseth thee" (Gen 12:3b)*. God is saying our enemies will become His enemies. He said it to Abraham, but the promises of Abraham also apply to us. *"Now to Abraham and his seed were the promises made" (Galations 3:16)*. You might say, "But that promise is to Abraham's children."—

"Ye are the children of the prophets, and of the covenant which God made with our fathers, saying unto Abraham, And in thy seed shall all the kindreds of the earth be blessed" (Acts 3:25). He also extended Abraham's promise to us.

God wants us to have His divine favor. He wants us to be able to see things as He sees them. He wants us to be able to see the outcome of our battles, even, when the clouds hide the sun. The devil tries to darken our nights before we realize it is only a cloud covering the sun like a curtain.

For Adam and Eve, the enemy schematically deceived her into thinking they needed spiritual insight for a better life (I Timothy 2:14). He tricked her into thinking they would be of better service if they ate the fruit. He showed them an opportunity to have spiritual insight beyond their physical eye. He enticed them by the glory of the fruit to commit a sin. The enemy knew that eating the fruit would anger God. Adam would receive spiritual insight, but the enemy knew Adam would receive spirit insight by being disobedient. He would receive spiritual insight by sinning. On account of Adam's sin we are born into sin, but we lack spiritual discernment.

Today the devil tries to do the exact opposite for our failure. The enemy tries to get us to sin to *keep us* from obtaining spiritual discernment. He tries to cause us to do other things to rebel against God. He understands that if we remain obedient to God while deepening our relationship with Him (God), that God will grant us some spiritual insight. *"The secret of the LORD is with them that fear (respect) him; he will shew them his covenant" (Psalms 25:14).* God will begin to show us things that He does not show others. The devil is afraid of this.

What he (devil) fears is for us to get into deep relationship with God, because God has a way of keeping His (God) believers. During our spiritual walk, God tends to lie presents alongside the road. He will allow us to experience His benefits. *"Blessed be the Lord, who daily loadeth us with benefits, even the God of our salvation" (Psalms 68:19).* The enemy knows there are benefits on God's side. He (devil) knows the longer you walk with God, the more detrimental you become to his (enemy's) kingdom. The enemy tries to expose us to things that appeal to our senses, things that are disobedient to what God instructs for us. Therefore, he tries to counteract God's benefits with his own. The enemy will help you get that good-looking boy/girl-man/woman that has no relationship with God. He (the enemy) knows they will help him open the space between you and God by leading you into rebellious acts. This is why having spiritual discernment to expose the enemy is critical.

God will, oftentimes, allow us to become

enticed to certain things to prove us. He wants us to prove our love for Him. He wants us to prove how serious we are about our relationship with Him. God will not allow us to be tempted without providing us an escape. *"There hath no temptation taken you but such as is common to man: but God [is] faithful, who will not suffer you to be tempted above that ye are able; but will with the temptation also make a way to escape, that ye may be able to bear [it]" (I Corinthians 10:13).* God will always warn us of danger before we fall. When the sirens go off, it is our job to take heed to the warning.

God will help us expose the enemy, before the enemy exposes us toward a sin he (the enemy) wants us to commit. If we pass the test we will move to a new spiritual level. We must expose the enemy before the sin becomes lodged inside our body, and he (the enemy) exposes us like he did Adam and Eve. Their sin exposed them to God. Be sure our sins will also expose us (see Numbers 32:23) if we don't expose him (the enemy) first.

Practical Principles

Romans 12:2

"And be not conformed to this world: but be ye transformed by the renewing of your mind, that ye may prove what is that good, and acceptable, and perfect, will of God."

We are constantly changing every second. Are you changing positively or negatively? It will do no good if your heart is sensitive to God, but your mind is not following suit. Our hearts and our minds must have some sort of flow. The Scripture tells us that our mind must be constantly renewed for us to transform into who He created us to be. Transformation is a process. Our spiritual transformation depends on the changing of the mind.

John 11:10

"But if a man walk in the night, he stumbleth, because there is no light in him."

Is your relationship with God deep enough for Him to expose the enemy and his (the enemy's) tactics to you? Jesus said He is the Light of the world. Based on the previous chapter, we already know how to "eat," Jesus (to draw from and be nourished by our relationship with Him). If Jesus is the light of the world, then Jesus will produce light inside us. Thus, we are required to deepen our spiritual relationship with God. Is God able to reveal to us the traps that are laid down for our failure, or is our relationship with God too shallow?

Summary Prayer

Dear Father - I pray that You would show me the way to transformation. I desire to become more appealing to You. I know that the enemy would love to separate me from learning of You.

There is no better time than now for me to be more serious about my relationship with You, God. Reveal the snares (traps) the enemy has laid down for me. Show me how to escape his (the enemy's) wrath. No weapon formed against me shall prevail. I will become what You say I will become. I give You my life. Help me deepen my relationship with You.

Chapter 10

Consummation

God has been so good to me through all the trials and tribulations I have encountered since the beginning of my life. It pays to be on this side of the fence. As I re-visit different stages of my life up to this point, I have reason to devote my whole life to God. I wonder if certain things would have taken place if I had never made the decision to live for God. I wonder if God would have told me He had a pre-pared place for me to stay in Maryland/D.C., or even if He would have *orchestrated* a place for me to stay. I question whether or not God would have placed certain people in my life to help me along the way. I have noticed through every struggle I have endured, God never let me see total destruction.

I cried, I whimpered, I begged, I moaned, I threw a few fits, but God never left me lonely. It took me a while to realize that He was in the battles with me, but I finally got the picture. That is what the enemy would love for us to think—he wants us to think that God is not real, or, if He (God) *is* real that

He does not care for us as much as people say He does. He wants us to feel neglected while we are in the battle. The enemy tries to use our battles to separate us from God and blind us from His true nature.

I cannot understand how people deny that God is real when life *defines* Him. I mean—through bright stars, the changes in the atmosphere, through mother nature, lullabies sung by whistling birds, breezy winds, through the beauty of mankind, the functioning of our body, and our own creative abilities. Who else could be responsible? We love to give credit elsewhere; that is until life starts it rampage over us by pushing us into a comfortless and unsatisfied situation. Then we decide to start a search for God. We wait until all else fails before we start a scavenger hunt for God.

We cannot let life back us deep in a corner, while the clock expires, before we acknowledge the realness of God. God is not some cheap Barbie doll, or heroic action figure that we can pick up among the isolated stages of our lives to feel a phony sense of comfort. God is more real than we give Him credit. God really does love us.

My mother once told me that she saw one of my brothers talking to God about his problems at age four. That almost seems preposterous; but it is true. I am talking about a child who did not grow up in a church, nor was taught to reverence God. We are discussing the age when a child's mind lacks the fabrication to comprehend what is evolving around them.

This young beautiful creation, my brother, acknowledged the realness of God before he could really understand God's sovereign power. Just thinking about that leaves me speechless. I never discussed it with him to see if he could remember it, but the thought of a four-year-old child reverencing God is overtaking. Now I understand why, even, he (my brother) has been wrestling with life since the day he was born. The enemy wants to agitate the perception he has of God.

The enemy hates for a person to reverence God. The closer we get, the more the enemy tries to shake us into a mental box of confusion. The enemy will try to make us second-guess our commitment to God. We will always have battles to fight. The only difference in being on God's side, and being without God, is that *we* will always come out of the battle victorious. God has always brought me out with a smile, more love, more patience, more care, more joy, more faith, and perfect peace after every fight. Without a relationship with God we are subject to search for love, patience, care, joy, and for peace in all the wrong places. Leaning on other people will leave us unfulfilled in the long run. *"Confidence in an unfaithful man in time of trouble [is like] a broken tooth, and a foot out of joint" (Proverbs 25:19).* This is one reason why people in marriages do not stay unified, why kids run away from home, why parents cannot cope with their family, and why people cannot survive life. They are looking for love in all the wrong places. Every place without God is unstable.

I was watching the news last night right after I started writing this chapter. They were talking about teenage girls who were living lives of prostitution; young women of all ages, races, and from different backgrounds. The reporter came to a conclusion why these young women were engaging in this activity. She reportedly asked the girls why they felt like they had to be prostitutes. She said all the answers were the same. They just wanted to be loved and feel wanted. All these girls are lost in the confinements of life while trying to find a fulfilling love.

One of my other brothers, who is an ordained minister, said something very profound. During one of his Sunday messages, he said God told him,

"You cannot love yourself or anyone else until you learn how to love the lover!"

It is imperative for us to learn how to *love the lover,* and then teach our children to do the same.

Who is this lover? The true lover is the one who gave His only Son to us. He is our God. We must learn how to love God, before true love is totally defined.

Benefits of a made decision

God has been affirming His promise to me since the day He spoke it. The misinterpretation to box His promise in and tie it to money is where I missed the mark. When I got the job at Goodyear Auto-care, God affirmed His promise in my life. When God established a resting place for me in Maryland/D.C., He defined His promise. The new friend that assisted me when I returned to Dallas helped fulfill His promise. I really could tell you many other things that define the grace God has given me. I am not being boastful. I am just thankful.

I want you to see some of the benefits we have through our relationship with God. God has always rewarded my faith. If I never had the sense to have faith in Him, He would not have acted on a lot of things. My faith is what moved God. My faith is the reason I left for Maryland/D.C. If I had not left Dallas, God would not have been able to use me like He wanted to in a new area. I also would have been short of one special family.

I am so glad I met the family I have in Maryland. God spoke a word that was contrary to my situation by telling me I had a place to stay. I found out God knew a secret that no one else knew but Him. Natural facts said I did not have a logical place to stay, but *God* said *I did.* All I had to do was believe. He let me in on the secret, which I have shared with you. Wouldn't you love to deepen your relationship with God where He is able to trust you enough with His secrets?

I believe all of us have told people we thought were our close friends, some of our secrets. The only thing with them is they could not conceal our business. Before we knew it everybody knew what our secrets were. The difference with God is He only tells *certain people* His secrets. We did not know we couldn't trust those people with our secrets until they revealed themselves to be phony friends. God knows exactly who He can tell His secrets to.

In the last chapter I told you, *"The secret of the LORD is with them that fear him; and he will shew them his covenants" (Psalms 25:14).* Fear in this usage means "to respect." How much do we fear, or respect God? Is our respect enough for Him to tell us His secrets? The New International Version bible, or NIV says, *"The LORD confides in those that fear him; he makes his covenant known to them" (Proverbs 25:14).*

Life is so much better for us when we have a friend that knows where all the treasure is. It is so much easier to live when someone is able to direct us down the right paths. *"The steps of a good man are ordered by the LORD: and he delighteth in his way" (Psalms 37:23).* God is a friend that knows who is hiring for new jobs, who to sign business contracts with, what doctors can really help, what counselors to talk to, what lawyers to depend on, what cars are dependable, what child to adopt, what person to marry, and what house to buy. *God has secrets.* The only way we can find out the secrets is by wooing Him, and proving ourselves faithful. He has to trust us with His secrets. He must believe we are dependable friends. Jesus said, *"Ye are my friends, if ye do whatsoever I command you. Henceforth I call you not servants; for the servant knoweth not what his lord doeth: but I have called you friends; for all things that I have heard of my Father I have made unto you" (John 15:14, 15).* Jesus called us his friends?

I know He declares us to be His friends, but are we *really* His friends? Is God able to whisper His secrets into our ears? Or, are we half stepping our way to Christianity? Are we Christians only on Sundays? Do we have enough faith in God to let go of things that keep us from living a life totally devoted to Him? God desires to bless us no matter where we are, or where we are going. He wants to show us that He has been in the boat during the entire storm, like He was with the disciples.

While Jesus and the disciples were on their way to the country of the Gadarenes, they ran into a tumultuous storm. The Bible says the storm was so drastic that the winds blew the waves from the sea into the ship. Jesus was at the bottom part of the ship resting. The disciples got weary of what was going on. They started to fear for their life. They looked over at Jesus, awoke him, and asked him if He cared that they were about to die. Jesus got up told the wind to cease its action, and commanded the sea to calm down. After the wind and sea obeyed His voice, He asked the disciples why they were so fearful (see Mark 4:37–39). Then He said to them, *"How is it that ye have no faith?" (Mark 4:40).*

This windstorm is a correlation of how we live our lives today. It takes more faith for us to believe that God is in the storm with us, because we do not have the benefit of physically seeing Jesus today like the disciples did yesterday. The disciples could look over at Jesus and physically ask Him for a response.

God is in every storm with us, but He might not

say a word until the appropriate time. He might not take action as quick as we want Him to; therefore, life makes Him seem absent. This is what connects many of the disciples' situations to ours.

Jesus was in the midst of the same battle as the disciples. He was, definitely, available for call. He did not jump up and act out of fear like everyone else on the boat, so it made Him seem carelessly absent. The disciples' situation clouded Jesus as being absent. They probably would have felt like they were alone if they did not have the benefit of looking directly at Him.

Even though Jesus was in the storm with them, He said something very intriguing. He asked them, "Where is your faith?" This is somewhat puzzling to me. It is puzzling, because I put myself into their situation. If a storm broke out, tossing water into my canoe, while I was in the middle of a sea, I would probably react much like they did. After waking Jesus up to hear Him ask me where my faith was, would leave me puzzled.

For Jesus to question their faith depicts the power that God has invested within us. It shows the benefit we have in Him. Jesus asked them a question that defines them as having the power through Him to do what He did. This transcends human nature. I ask myself, "Whether or not Jesus is telling us that we have a benefit of speaking to things that have no ears to hear?"

That is exactly what He is saying. Jesus was telling His disciples to *activate their faith* for the pur-

Demetrius Smith

pose of survival. Do you think that God is careless enough to let the storm kill you?

I don't! As a matter of fact, I have been speaking to earless situations for some time now. All I know is there are benefits through having faith in God.

More than Much

Can you fathom being center stage of a sea where you are the focal point of hellish commotion? Would you understand being in the middle of a roaring storm, on a boat, with dashes of water carelessly evading your territory, not knowing if you will survive the catastrophe, and look over to witness your friend act as if nothing was wrong? My friend, Jesus was in the middle of a similar situation; asleep!

Jesus was conclusively the ultimate teacher for our lives. He knew some things about God that were incomprehensible. Jesus was so uncompromisingly compatible with God that death threats, or even death itself, could not separate Him from the reality of God. Jesus understood the severity of His faith in God. He knew the importance of His survival depended on God. His relationship with God was so pure that a situation described at the beginning of this section was incapable of moving Him. The disciples were afraid, but Jesus was not. Jesus continued to weather the storm through God's perfect peace.

Jesus exemplified a man who knew why He was on earth. He showed us that in understanding who we are in Him (Jesus), we do not have to fear the trials of life. I recall a cliché one of my sisters often said. She would come into the house and tell us who tried to pick a fight with her. She would briefly describe the story, and tell us how they threatened her. Then, she would end with, "I told her, 'I ain't losing no sleep over you!'"

Jesus was not losing any sleep at the hands of a death threat. The storm was loudly roaring, but Jesus was quietly sleeping. Jesus showed us the effectiveness that our relationship can have with Him. First, He *showed* us. Then, He *told* us.

He told us to, *"Come unto me, all ye that labour and are heavy laden, and I will give you rest" (Matthew 11:28)*. The NIV gives us a clearer understanding of this Scripture. It says, *"Come to me, all you who are weary and burdened, and I will give you rest" (Matthew 11:28)*. In verse 27 of Matthew, Jesus said, *"All things are delivered unto me of my father: and no man knows the Son, but the Father; neither knoweth any man the Father, save (except) the Son, and he to whomever the Son will reveal him" (Matthew 11:27)*. Jesus drew His rest from God. We are to draw our rest from Jesus; nevertheless, we are also drawing it from God. He will give us incomprehensible rest through our situations.

We do not have to lose anymore sleep on behalf of the turmoil we go through. If we really understood God, and who we are in Him by Jesus, we would not fret at every situation. We do not have to fear the worst from every storm we encounter. This is another reason why getting a deeper revelation of who God is means *more than much*. If you ever understand how valuable a promise from God is; you should have no problem with wavering faith, or lack of faith. If you ever find out the secret of God, and His revealed promises to you; then life will have no vote on your destiny. The disciples that were in the storm with Jesus did not thoroughly understand the promises they could obtain.

When Jesus took the disciples into the mountains to teach them, one of the things He told them was He had to fulfill prophecy (see Matthew 5:17). One of God's prophets was Zechariah. Zechariah prophesied the aftermath of the crucifixion (see Zechariah 12:10). If the disciples knew the prophecy, and understood the depth of the prophecy, they would have known they had a walking promise with them. What Zechariah prophesied was one of the prophecies Jesus had to fulfill. The circumstance Jesus and the disciples were involved in washed the disciples into a faithless mindset.

If Jesus had to fulfill a prophecy of being crucified, that meant nothing could happen to the boat they were in. The situation they were in at that time spoke death. The promise they had with them was Jesus fulfilling prophecy. This tells me that the promise they had with them was speaking something contrary to what they were facing. *Their situation spoke death, but the promise spoke life.* Jesus could not die at the hands of a sinking boat.

Jesus also had a promise that He would not die except by the hands of men, only to resurrect from death days later. If the disciples knew the promise they had with them they would have known that the storm *had* to pass. Jesus knew the promise He had; which allowed Him to *rest through the storm* and allow it to pass. He got up to impede the storms action, because of the fearful disciples. *If we get a promise from God, we cannot die until the prophecy is fulfilled.* If we lack the faith to speak to the storm, at least, we need to have enough faith in God to weather the storm until it passes over. God promised us peace that passes our understanding while we are weathering the storm, if we talk to Him about it (see Philippians 4:7).

Lock into God through faith, and watch Him fulfill His promises. *God is more than much,* and believing in Him is the basis for gathering more information from Him.

Fulfilling the Beginning

"You shall be prosperous all the days of your life" is what God told me. God will always have a purpose for any promise that He gives us. My job is to find out the complete reason for Him speaking such a promise to me. One reason is for Kingdom building. I have shared a small proportion of my life to help re-energize you for the battles you face, and for the battles you will face ahead. I know we do not like to talk about future battles, but we must not be surprised at the things we have to overcome. If we are aware of them, then we have the opportunity to prepare for them.

God can use anyone of us. We have to remain available for the call. I dare to say that all of us have been walking in a face of God's prosperity. We have been walking in His mercy since we entered into this world. As a matter of fact, we met His mercy while we were in our mother's womb. Some children did not make it out of the womb. We made it out, so that alone is enough to be thankful for. We wake up in God's mercy. Then we walk in His mercy.

It would shock us if we found out what the devil really wanted to do to us. We would be amazed once we discovered the limits God puts on the enemy regarding our lives. *There is not one thing you face that you are not strong enough to survive.* There is a purpose for you being in the situation that you are in. The battle you face was designed specifically for you to conquer it. You might question why it could not be another person dealing with your struggles, but "that someone else" might not be fit enough to deal with what you are dealing with. I do not know if I would be living if I had to fight an excessive drug addiction. God chose me to battle some other things. I would probably lose my mind if I were an addict.

Contrarily, an addict may not be able to survive another person's storms. If you are dealing with a drug addiction, you can beat the system of relapses. You can overcome your struggles. The key to being victorious is making a decision not to fail within your heart. Whatever you are battling, victory must be decided *in your heart.* God knows what situations best suit you for growth. God knows what situations are fit for us to encounter. He does not put evil on us, but He *allows* certain things to happen to us for a reason.

On the other hand, there are certain things God

kept from appearing in our paths. He placed His hand between you and certain things the devil desired to do to you. We will begin to understand that we are prosperous people once we realize the grace God has given to us.

God passionately cares for all of us. It took God's love to adopt people like myself into His royal family. You are no different from me. Like I stated earlier, even if you are not a full-fledged Christian, God sheltered you from some things. God wants to adopt whosoever will come. That is why He saved us from certain things. How can we not serve the Creator who blesses His people, and His enemies? *"He maketh his sun to rise on the evil and the good, and sendeth rain on the just and on the unjust" (Matthew 5:45).* It is almost absurd for God to bless both. We definitely care less about blessing anyone we consider our enemy. This Scripture defines the grace God has bestowed upon us.

God could snatch His hand back at any time, and allow the enemy to run ballistic over our lives if He preferred. Let's not take things for granted. Lets find a deeper revelation of God than that we currently have of Him. Let's deepen our faith, and pray more fervently to God. *"Confess your faults one to another, and pray one for another, that ye may be healed. The effectual fervent prayer of a righteous man availeth much" (James 5:16).* God is able to deliver us from whatever we are dealing with.

If we have been leaning on Him, and He has not delivered us yet; chances are we still have enough gas in the tank to make it through. If we run out of gas, God will drag us through it if He has to. God will not let us see total destruction, provided we keep depending on Him. We must grab hold of enough faith to speak to our earless situations. The psalmist declared, *"I will not die, but live, and declare the works of the LORD" (Psalms 118:17).* What is your declaration?

Will you let your situation pump the last gasp of air out of you? Or, will you live and not die to declare the works of the LORD?

We must not let the enemy cloud our perception from the realness of God. As we grow, we should realize that we are wealthier than we ever imagined, despite our situation.

We literally grow older in age every second. As we grow old we are physically dying. We might appear physically beautiful, but our outer encasement is dying. We do everything we can imagine to dress up our outer being. We have makeovers, plastic surgery, stitch in new hair, lift weights, adjust our facial expressions, and whatever else we can think of to enhance our beauty. We perform these works to improve our physical glory even though we are dying. *"FOR ALL FLESH IS AS GRASS AND ALL THE GLORY OF MAN AS THE FLOWER OF GRASS. THE GRASS WITHERETH, AND THE FLOWER THEREOF FALLEY AWAY:" (I Peter 2:24).* We are dying, and we have no choice; we can thank Adam for that.

Jesus gave us the command to die in another sense; die to our own passions. He commanded us to take up our cross and walk. For us to take up our cross, and die to ourselves has to happen by choice. This signifies two different ways of death: a law of death, and a self-willed death.

There is no justification for what Adam did, but God in His awesomeness has the tendency to work all things out for our good (Romans 8:28). We can thank Adam for the dying process, but we have an opportunity to see with a spiritual eye. We can thank God for that. Adam brought death upon us, but in doing so he also allowed us the *spiritual* insight that is necessary for us today. The upside is that God gave us the benefit of spiritual insight on our way to death. Then came Jesus!

Jesus perfected the spiritual insight with a benefit of eternal life through the spirit. God made our spirit. *"The burden of the word of the LORD for Israel, saith the LORD, which stretcheth forth the heavens, and layeth the foundation of the earth, and formeth the spirit of man within him" (Zechariah 12:1).* Everything that God has given me to say in this book is designed to help strengthen our spiritual man, and stir up our faith. It is food for our spirit. God gives us an opportunity to see Him in a deeper perspective.

We must adhere to His offer. We will find ourselves learning more about God when we talk to Him, worship Him, praise Him, and honor Him. We will also learn more about who we are as His loving creation. Though our bodies are constantly dying, we should be unceasingly growing spiritually. We live in a carcass of poverty. Our *spirit is the wealthiest part of our body.* The more we feed our God-created spirit the wealthier we will become spiritually. As we continuously feed our spirit, God will constantly reveal more of Himself to us.

God chose our body in which to dwell. He gives us the opportunity to sow to the spirit what He has invested within us. It is not that God is lacking, or needs more substance to grow. God does not need to grow, because He is God. *He is already large and in charge.* We need to grow to match the spirit He is inside of us. It is as if He has a quilt over Himself while living inside of us. As we sow to our spirit, He reveals more of Himself to us. God pulls the quilt off of Himself; bit by bit, when we spend time doing things that nourish our spirit. Therefore, it appears as if our spirit is growing.

If we learn how to walk in the spirit, we will learn how to walk in His prosperous paths. Our bodies benefit nothing in the Kingdom of God. Our *spirit* is amazingly wealthy in the Kingdom. Our spirit is a priceless gem in the Kingdom. It defines the word wealthy in every facet.

God is that spirit. Our God owns everything from healing to money to being victorious. Our faith in Jesus, by way of the Spirit, locks us into God. Faith is what qualifies us to obtain the benefits of God. The same faith fuels us to overcome our battles. Our superior God wants our life totally. Welcoming our superior God into our bodies increases our value as His people. He will lead us to victory over our problems. *"Now thanks be unto God, which always causeth us to triumph in Christ" (2 Corinthians 2:14a).* The simple fact that our God chose our impoverished bodies as His temple tells me that we are *"Wealthy in a Poverty Estate!"*

Practical Principles

John 7:38

"He that believeth on me, as the scripture hath said, out of his belly shall flow rivers of living waters."

I need you to ponder on this Scripture for a moment. Doesn't that sound refreshing . . .rivers of living waters?!!

I envision an awesome waterfall with crystal clear water that is more refreshing than ice cold tea on a hot scorching summer day. This scriptural waterbrook has the ability to flow unhindered. The waters that depart from the fountain of our belly are rivers of living waters.

The Scripture depicts a spiritual flow of the spirit that resembles a physical flow of water. Scientific facts state that our body is made up of mostly water. We are supposed to drink eight cups of water on a daily basis. If our body is made up of water, it makes sense to keep our body filled with water. Just as your body is dominated by water, your body should also be filled with the Holy Spirit.

The Scripture says that from our "belly shall flow rivers of living water." Water is a cleansing agent. It is a sign of new birth, it is a thirst quencher, and it is a dominant source for survival. We have this agent flowing inside of us based on a spiritual perspective. Drink from the waterbrook that will quench all of your needs, wants, and desires. The flowing river will help keep you cleansed from filth. It will also comfort you in desperate situations.

Galatians 6: 8, 9

"For he that soweth to his flesh shall of the flesh reap corruption; but he that soweth to the Spirit shall of the Spirit reap life everlasting. And let us not be weary in well doing: for in due season we shall reap, if we faint not."

The last person God showed me to write these words to was dealing with battles on her job. God directed me to share this information with her. The next thing I knew she got a new job offer while people were losing jobs. Isn't is funny how God works?

God would not allow me to finish this book with any other Scripture. I leave you with a command to stay strong, and to be encouraged. Do not worry about anything that you are going through. That is exactly what you are doing; you are *"going through"* a battle. You will not stay in the battle. So do not faint.

Whatever you want in life, sow seeds to reap a harvest on your expectation. If you want deliverance, sow seeds toward your deliverance. God knows exactly what we are in need of, but He also expects us to act on our faith!

Summary Prayer

Dear Father, I come in the name of the everlasting King Jesus. I ask that You will help me to learn how to drink from the river that never runs dry. I pray that You would strengthen me as I walk the course of my life. Grant me peace of mind from unstable weariness. I pray for an increase in my faith to believe in You. Ignite me to develop a deeper passion for You. I want to be more like You. Grant me Your divine favor, and help me to remain humble. I will overcome; I can overcome, because I am a conqueror in Jesus name. Amen!

Contact Demetrius Smith
or order more copies of this book at

TATE PUBLISHING, LLC

127 East Trade Center Terrace
Mustang, Oklahoma 73064

(888) 361 - 9473

Tate Publishing, LLC

www.tatepublishing.com